Machine Learning with Qlik Sense

Utilize different machine learning models in practical use cases by leveraging Qlik Sense

Hannu Ranta

BIRMINGHAM—MUMBAI

Machine Learning with Qlik Sense

Group Product Manager: Ali Abidi

Publishing Product Manager: Sanjana Gupta

Book Project Manager: Farheen Fathima

Content Development Editor: Joseph Sunil

Technical Editor: Devanshi Ayare

Copy Editor: Safis Editing

Proofreader: Safis Editing

Indexer: Hemangini Bari

Production Designer: Prashant Ghare

DevRel Marketing Coordinator: Vinishka Kalra

First published: October 2023

Production reference: 1290923

Published by Packt Publishing Ltd.

Grosvenor House

11 St Paul's Square

Birmingham

B3 1RB, UK.

ISBN 978-1-80512-615-7

www.packtpub.com

To my parents for the support and encouragement during my life.
To Essi for being my dive buddy in life.

-Hannu Ranta

Contributors

About the author

Hannu Ranta is a data and cloud professional with wide technical knowledge. He has worked with big data, IoT, and analytics solutions with the largest enterprises across the globe. He always enjoys finding innovative solutions to build a better future with data, while helping customers to deliver value.

Hannu obtained his Master of Science degree with distinction in 2015 and has worked for leading data companies like Qlik, Microsoft and Cubiq Analytics since then. Currently, he is a Principal Enterprise Architect for Nordic and Baltic region at Qlik.

When not working, Hannu is usually scuba diving, snowboarding, or traveling. Originally from Tammela, Finland, he now lives in Helsinki, the capital of Finland, with his girlfriend.

I want to thank my girlfriend, Essi, for the support and encouragement during the writing process and my parents for everything. I would also like to thank my colleagues from Qlik for all the help and support, especially Troels, Mikko, and the Finnish team. Thanks also to my friends, for inspiring conversations, and everyone else who helped me during my career.

About the reviewers

Rohan Chikorde is an accomplished AI Architect professional with a post-graduate in Machine Learning and Artificial Intelligence. With almost a decade of experience, he has successfully developed NLP, Deep Learning and Machine Learning models for various business applications. Rohan's expertise spans multiple domains, and he excels in programming languages such as R and Python, as well as analytics techniques like regression analysis and data mining. In addition to his technical prowess, he is an effective communicator, mentor, and team leader. Rohan's passion lies in machine learning, deep learning, and computer vision.

Thank you so much to the Packt team for the opportunity.

Pablo Labbe is a seasoned consultant working on Business Intelligence (BI) projects over 25 years. During his journey he was always challenged to help organizations to be more data-driven. He is currently a Principal Solution Architect at iMaps Intelligence, a data and analytics company located in Brazil South Region.

Pablo has leveraged his expertise by directly working within industries such as government, retail, healthcare, agriculture, and manufacturing.

Pablo is the co-author of two books related to Qlik Sense: Qlik Sense Cookbook, 2nd edition and Hands-On Business Intelligence with Qlik Sense.

Clever Anjos is a Principal Solutions Architect at Qlik, a data analytics and data integration software company. He has been working for Qlik since 2018 but has been around the Qlik Ecosystem as a Partner and Customer since 2009. He is a Business Discovery professional with several years of experience working with Qlik, AWS, Google Cloud, Databricks, and other BI technologies.

He is a highly active member of the Qlik Community, with over 8,000 posts and 4.5K page views. In May 2022, he was named the Qlik Community's Featured Member. Clever is also a writer and has published a book called *Hands-On Business Intelligence With Qlik*.

Table of Contents

Part 2: Machine learning algorithms and models with Qlik

Part 3: Case studies and best practices

10

Examples and Case Studies   187

11

Future Direction   205

Index   213

Other Books You May Enjoy   222

Preface

Machine Learning with Qlik Sense is a book for anyone who wants to master machine learning and expand their use of analytics into predictive use cases. You will learn the key concepts of machine learning using practical examples, enabling you to create better analytics applications and get the most out of your data.

Qlik Sense is a world-leading data analytics platform with comprehensive capabilities in machine learning. This book will guide you to build machine learning enabled analytics solutions using both Qlik Cloud Analytics with AutoML and Qlik Sense Client-Managed.

Who this book is for

If you are interested in data and analytics with a will to extend your skillset to machine learning, this book is for you. In order to learn from this book, you should have basic knowledge of working with data, preferably with Qlik tools. This book is an excellent guide for everyone willing to take the next step on their journey and start using machine learning as a part of their data analytics journey.

What this book covers

Chapter 1, Introduction to Machine Learning with Qlik, will introduce you to the world of machine learning with the Qlik platform. This chapter covers all the basic concepts for implementing machine learning with Qlik, like R2, F1 and SHAP.

Chapter 2, Machine Learning Algorithms and Models with Qlik, will provide information about the essential algorithms and models in machine learning focusing on ones important in the Qlik platform. You will get a basic understanding of how the algorithms behind Qlik's ML solution work and how to pick the right one for specific problems.

Chapter 3, Data Literacy in a Machine Learning Context, will cover how data literacy can be utilized in a machine learning context. You will learn and utilize data literacy skills to get the most out of the data that ML models are using.

Chapter 4, Creating a Good Machine Learning Solution with the Qlik Platform, covers the essential knowledge to create a good machine learning solution with the Qlik platform. You will learn all the steps needed to utilize automated solutions for model building.

Chapter 5, Setting Up the Environments, teaches how to set up the environments for machine learning using Qlik tools. You will get hands on examples for setting up and initializing different environments and also cover any problems that might occur during the setup, and how to fix them.

Chapter 6, Preprocessing and Exploring Data with Qlik Sense, will cover the techniques needed to preprocess the data in Qlik Sense. This chapter will guide you through all the important steps for preprocessing and exploring data. You will learn how to validate data and make data exploration efficient.

Chapter 7, Deploying and Monitoring Machine Learning Models, will cover how to deploy and monitor machine learning models in both cloud and client-managed environments. It will also cover what to consider before deploying to production.

Chapter 8, Utilizing Qlik AutoML, covers the use of Qlik AutoML tool in both cloud and on-premise environments. This chapter will guide you with the best practices and features of AutoML using real-world examples. You will also learn the features of AutoML and models that can be deployed using the tool.

Chapter 9, Advanced Data Visualization Techniques for Machine Learning Solutions, provides examples and best practices about visualizing machine learning related data with Qlik tools. This chapter covers Qlik charts and advanced features and functions to fully utilize the charts. It will also cover how to use Insight Advisor to help visualization tasks and provide insights about data.

Chapter 10, Examples and Case Studies, guides you through real world examples and use cases with Qlik's machine learning portfolio. Each example is described in detailed level and also the information about the business value is provided.

Chapter 11, Future Direction, will give you an idea of the future development and trends of machine learning. You will get information about overall trends and how the Qlik portfolio will develop to support the adoption of new trends.

To get the most out of this book

You should have basic knowledge of Qlik tools and data analytics to get the most out of this book. Also, basic knowledge of Qlik Cloud and AutoML and understanding the basic machine learning concepts and statistics is helpful.

Software/hardware covered in the book	Operating system requirements
Qlik Cloud Analytics and Qlik AutoML	
Qlik Sense Client Managed or Qlik Sense Desktop	Windows
R and RStudio	Windows
Python	Windows

If you are using the digital version of this book, we advise you to type the code yourself or access the code from the book's GitHub repository (a link is available in the next section). Doing so will help you avoid any potential errors related to the copying and pasting of code.

Download the example code files

You can download the example code files for this book from GitHub at `https://github.com/ PacktPublishing/Machine-Learning-with-Qlik-Sense`. If there's an update to the code, it will be updated in the GitHub repository.

We also have other code bundles from our rich catalog of books and videos available at `https:// github.com/PacktPublishing/`. Check them out!

Conventions used

There are a number of text conventions used throughout this book.

`Code in text`: Indicates code words in text, database table names, folder names, filenames, file extensions, pathnames, dummy URLs, user input, and Twitter handles. Here is an example: "Mount the downloaded `WebStorm-10*.dmg` disk image file as another disk in your system."

A block of code is set as follows:

```
iris:
LOAD
RowNo() as id,
    sepal_length,
    sepal_width,
    petal_length,
    petal_width
FROM [lib://<PATH TO DATAFILE>/iris_test.csv]
(txt, utf8, embedded labels, delimiter is ',', msq);
```

When we wish to draw your attention to a particular part of a code block, the relevant lines or items are set in bold:

```
[predictions]:
LOAD * EXTENSION endpoints.ScriptEval('{"RequestType":"endpoint",
"endpoint":{"connectionname":"ML demos:Iris"}}', iris);
```

Bold: Indicates a new term, an important word, or words that you see onscreen. For instance, words in menus or dialog boxes appear in **bold**. Here is an example: " If we would like to change our experiment, we can select **Configure v2**".

> **Tips or important notes**
> Appear like this.

Get in touch

Feedback from our readers is always welcome.

General feedback: If you have questions about any aspect of this book, email us at customercare@packtpub.com and mention the book title in the subject of your message.

Errata: Although we have taken every care to ensure the accuracy of our content, mistakes do happen. If you have found a mistake in this book, we would be grateful if you would report this to us. Please visit www.packtpub.com/support/errata and fill in the form.

Piracy: If you come across any illegal copies of our works in any form on the internet, we would be grateful if you would provide us with the location address or website name. Please contact us at copyright@packtpub.com with a link to the material.

If you are interested in becoming an author: If there is a topic that you have expertise in and you are interested in either writing or contributing to a book, please visit authors.packtpub.com.

Share Your Thoughts

Once you've read *Machine Learning with Qlik Sense*, we'd love to hear your thoughts! Scan the QR code below to go straight to the Amazon review page for this book and share your feedback.

https://packt.link/r/1-805-12615-6

Your review is important to us and the tech community and will help us make sure we're delivering excellent quality content.

Download a free PDF copy of this book

Thanks for purchasing this book!

Do you like to read on the go but are unable to carry your print books everywhere? Is your eBook purchase not compatible with the device of your choice?

Don't worry, now with every Packt book you get a DRM-free PDF version of that book at no cost.

Read anywhere, any place, on any device. Search, copy, and paste code from your favorite technical books directly into your application.

The perks don't stop there, you can get exclusive access to discounts, newsletters, and great free content in your inbox daily

Follow these simple steps to get the benefits:

1. Scan the QR code or visit the link below

https://packt.link/free-ebook/978-1-80512-615-7

2. Submit your proof of purchase

3. That's it! We'll send your free PDF and other benefits to your email directly

Part 1: Concepts of Machine Learning

This section will provide the background for the remaining parts of the book. The section covers the basics of machine learning with the Qlik platform and provides an understanding of important concepts and algorithms used in machine learning and statistics. It also covers the use of data literacy in the area of machine learning. Finally, this section provides the essentials of building a good machine learning solution with the Qlik platform. These concepts will be utilized during section 2 of this book.

This section has the following chapters:

- *Chapter 1: Introduction to Machine Learning with Qlik*
- *Chapter 2: Machine Learning Algorithms and Models with Qlik*
- *Chapter 3: Data Literacy in a Machine Learning Context*
- *Chapter 4: Creating a Good Machine Learning Solution with the Qlik Platform*

1

Introduction to Machine Learning with Qlik

Machine learning and artificial intelligence are two of the most powerful technology trends in the 21st century. Usage of these technologies is rapidly growing since the need for faster insights and forecasts has become crucial for companies. Qlik is a leading vendor in the analytics space and has heavily invested in machine learning and AI tools.

This first chapter will introduce the different machine learning tools in the Qlik ecosystem and provide basic information about the statistical models and principles behind these tools. It will also cover the concepts of correct sample size and how to analyze model performance and reliability.

Here is what we will cover in this first chapter:

- An overview of the Qlik tools and platform
- The basic statistical concepts of machine learning
- Proper sample size and the defining factors of a sample
- How to evaluate model performance and reliability

Introduction to Qlik tools

Qlik Sense is a leading data analytics and business intelligence platform and contains many tools and features for data analytics relating to machine learning. In this chapter, we will take a closer look at the key features of the Qlik platform.

Machine learning and AI capabilities on the Qlik platform can be divided into three different components:

- Insight Advisor
- Qlik AutoML
- Advanced Analytics Integration

Insight Advisor

Qlik Insight Advisor is a feature of Qlik Sense that uses **natural language processing** (**NLP**) and machine learning to help users explore and analyze data more effectively. It allows users to ask questions about their data in natural language and to receive insights and recommendations in real time. It also auto-generates advanced analytics and visualizations and assists with analytics creation and data preparation.

Insight Advisor utilizes a combination of Qlik's associative engine and augmented intelligence engine and supports a wide range of use cases, as seen in the following figure:

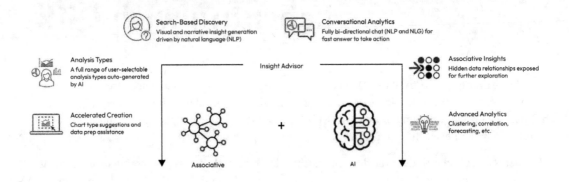

Figure 1.1: Qlik Insight Advisor and different scenarios

> **Did you know?**
>
> The Qlik associative engine is the core technology that powers the Qlik data analytics and business intelligence platform. It is a powerful in-memory engine that uses an associative data model, which allows users to explore data in a way that is more intuitive and natural than traditional query-based tools.
>
> Instead of pre-defined queries or data models, the engine automatically associates data across multiple tables and data sources based on common fields or attributes and uses a patented indexing technology that stores all the data in memory, enabling real-time analysis and exploration of even the largest datasets. It is a powerful and innovative technology that underpins the entire Qlik platform.

Insight Advisor has the following key features:

- **Advanced insight generation**: Insight Advisor provides a way to surface new and hidden insights. It uses AI-generated analyses that are delivered in multiple forms. Users can select from a full range of analysis types, which are auto-generated. These types include visualizations, narrative insights, and entire dashboards. Advanced analytics is also supported, and Insight Advisor can generate comparison, ranking, trending, clustering, geographical analysis, time series forecasts, and more.

- **Search-based visual discovery**: Insight Advisor auto-generates the most relevant and impactful visualizations for the users, based on natural language queries. It provides a set of charts that users can edit and fine-tune before adding to the dashboard. It is context-aware and reflects the selections with generated visualizations. It also suggests the most significant data relationships to explore further.

- **Conversational analytics**: Conversational analytics in Insight Advisor allows users to interact using natural language. Insight Advisor Chat offers a fully conversational analytics experience for the entire Qlik platform. It understands user intent and delivers additional insights for deeper understanding.

- **Accelerated creation and data preparation**: Accelerated creation and data preparation helps users to create analytics using a traditional build process. It gives recommendations about associations and relationships in data. It also gives chart suggestions and renders the best types of visualizations for each use case, which allows non-technical users to get the most out of the analyzed data. Part of the data preparation also involves an intelligent profiling that provides descriptive statistics about the data.

> **Note**
> A hands-on example with Insight Advisor can be found in *Chapter 9*, where you will be given a practical example of the most important functionalities in action.

Qlik AutoML

Qlik AutoML is an automated machine learning tool that makes AI-generated machine learning models and predictive analytics available for all users. It allows users to easily generate machine learning models, make predictions, and plan decisions using an intuitive, code-free user interface.

AutoML connects and profiles data, identifies key drivers in the dataset, and generates and refines models. It allows users to create future predictions and test what-if scenarios. Results are returned with prediction-influencer data (Shapley values) at the record level, which allows users to understand why predictions were made. This is critical to take the correct actions based on the outcome.

Predictive data can be published in Qlik Sense for further analysis and models can be integrated using Advanced Analytics Integration for real-time exploratory analysis.

Using AutoML is simple and does not require comprehensive data science skills. Users must first select the target field and then AutoML will run through various steps, as seen in the following figure:

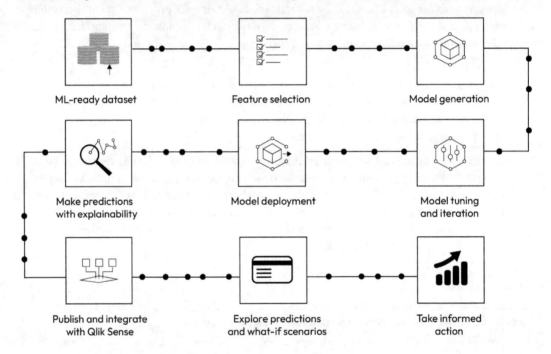

Figure 1.2: The AutoML process flow

With the model established and trained, AutoML lets users make predictions on current datasets. Deployed models can be used both from Qlik tools and other analytics tools. AutoML also provides a REST API to consume the deployed models.

> **Note**
> More information about AutoML, including hands-on examples, can be found in *Chapter 8*.

Advanced Analytics Integration

Advanced Analytics Integration is the ability to integrate advanced analytics and machine learning models directly into the Qlik data analytics platform. This integration allows users to combine the power of advanced analytics with the data exploration and visualization capabilities of Qlik to gain deeper insights from their data.

Advanced Analytics Integration is based on open APIs that provide direct, engine-level integration between Qlik's Associative Engine and third-party data science tools. Data is being exchanged and calculations are made in real time as the user interacts with the software. Only relevant data is passed from the Associative Engine to third-party tools, based on user selections and context. The workflow is explained in the following figure:

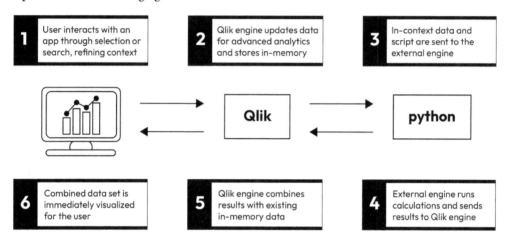

Figure 1.3: Advanced analytics integration dataflow

Advanced analytics integration can be used with any external calculation engine, but native connectivity is provided for Amazon SageMaker, Amazon Comprehend, Azure ML, Data Robot, and custom models made with R and Python. Qlik AutoML can also utilize advanced analytics integration.

> **Note**
>
> More information, including practical examples about advanced analytics integration, can be found in *Chapter 7*. Installing the needed components for the on-premises environment is described in *Chapter 5*.

Basic statistical concepts with Qlik solutions

Now that we have been introduced to Qlik tools, we will explore some of the statistical concepts that are used with them. Statistical principles play a crucial role in the development of machine-learning algorithms. These principles provide the mathematical framework for analyzing and modeling data, making predictions, and improving the accuracy of machine-learning models over time. In this section, we will become familiar with some of the key concepts that will be needed when building machine-learning solutions.

Types of data

Different data types are handled differently, and each requires different techniques. There are two major data types in typical machine-learning solutions: categorical and numerical.

Categorical data typically defines a group or category using a name or a label. Each piece of a categorical dataset is assigned to only one category and each category is mutually exclusive. Categorical data can be further divided into nominal data and ordinal data. Nominal data is the data category that names or labels a category. Ordinal data is constructed from elements with rankings, orders, or rating scales. Ordinal data can be ordered or counted but not measured. Some machine-learning algorithms can't handle categorical variables unless these are converted (encoded) to numerical values.

Numerical data can be divided into discrete data that is countable numerical data. It is formed using natural numbers, for example, age, number of employees in a company, etc. Another form of numerical data is continuous data. An example of this type of data can be a person's height or a student's score. One type of data to pay attention to is datetime information. Dates and times are typically useful in machine-learning models but will require some work to turn them into numerical data.

Mean, median, and mode

The **mean** is calculated by dividing the sum of all values in a dataset by the number of values. The simplified equation can be formed like this:

$$mean = \frac{Sum\ of\ all\ datapoints}{Number\ of\ datapoints}$$

The following is a simple example to calculate the mean of a set of data points:

$X = [5,15,30,45,50]$

$\bar{X} = (5+15+30+45+50)/5$

$\bar{X} = 29$

The mean is sensitive to outliers and these can significantly affect its value. The mean is typically written as $\bar{X}$.

The **median** is the middle value of the sorted dataset. Using the dataset in the previous example, our median is 30. The main advantage of the median over the mean is that the median is less affected by outliers. If there is a high chance for outliers, it's better to use the median instead of the mean. If we have an even number of data points in our dataset, the median is the average of two middle points.

The **mode** represents the most common value in a dataset. It is mostly used when there is a need to understand clustering or, for example, encoded categorical data. Calculating the mode is quite simple. First, we need to order all values and count how many times each value appears in a set. The value that appears the most is the mode. Here is a simple example:

$X = [1,4,4,5,7,9]$

The mode = 4 since it appears two times and all other values appear only one time. A dataset can also have multiple modes (multimodal dataset). In this case, two or more values occur with the highest frequency.

Variance

Variance ($\sigma2$) is a statistical measure that describes the degree of variability or spread in a set of data. It is the average of the squared differences from the mean of the dataset.

In other words, variance measures how much each data point deviates from the mean of the dataset. A low variance indicates that the data points are closely clustered around the mean, while a high variance indicates that the data points are more widely spread out from the mean.

The formula for variance is as follows:

$$\sigma^2 = \frac{\Sigma \left(x_i - \bar{x}\right)^2}{n - 1}$$

where $\sigma2$ is the variance of the dataset, n is the number of data points in the set, and Σ is the sum of the squared differences between each data point (xi) and the mean ($\bar{x}$). The square root of the variance is the standard deviation.

Variance is an important concept in statistics and machine learning, as it is used in the calculation of many other statistical measures, including standard deviation and covariance. It is also commonly used to evaluate the performance of models and to compare different datasets.

Variance is used to see how individual values relate to each other within a dataset. The advantage is that variance treats all deviations from the mean as the same, regardless of direction.

Example

We have a stock that returns 15% in year 1, 25% in year 2, and -10% in year 3. The mean of the returns is 10%. The difference of each year's return to mean is 5%, 15%, and -20%. Squaring these will give 0.25%, 2.25%, and 4%. If we add these together, we will get 6.5%. When divided by 2 (3 observations – 1), we get a variance of 3.25%.

Standard deviation

Standard deviation is a statistical measure that quantifies the amount of variation or dispersion in a set of data. It measures how much the individual data points deviate from the mean of the dataset.

A low standard deviation indicates that the data points are close to the mean, while a high standard deviation indicates that the data points are more spread out from the mean.

The formula for standard deviation is as follows:

$$\sigma = \sqrt{\frac{\Sigma\,(x_i - \bar{x})^2}{n - 1}}$$

where σ is the standard deviation, Σ is the sum of the squared differences between each data point (xi), and the mean ($\bar{x}$), and n is the number of data points.

> **Example**
>
> Continuing from our previous example, we got the variance of 3.25% for our stock. Taking the square root of the variance yields a standard deviation of 18%.

Standardization

Standardization or **Z-score normalization** is the concept of normalizing different variables to the same scale. This method allows comparison of scores between different types of variables. Z-score is a fractional representation of standard deviations from the mean value. We can calculate the z-score using the following formula:

$$z = \frac{x - \bar{x}}{\sigma}$$

In the formula, x is the observed value, $\bar{x}$ is the mean, and σ is the standard deviation of the data.

Basically, the z-score describes how many standard deviations away a specific data point is from the mean. If the z-score of a data point is high, it indicates that the data point is most likely an outlier. Z-score normalization is one of the most popular feature-scaling techniques in data science and is an important preprocessing step. Many machine-learning algorithms attempt to find trends in data and compare features of data points. It is problematic if features are on a different scales, which is why we need standardization.

> **Note**
>
> Standardized datasets will have a mean of 0 and standard deviation of 1, but there are no specific boundaries for maximum and minimum values.

Correlation

Correlation is a statistical measure that describes the relationship between two variables. It measures the degree to which changes in one variable are associated with changes in another variable.

There are two types of correlation: positive and negative. Positive correlation means that the two variables move in the same direction, while negative correlation means that the two variables move in opposite directions. A correlation of 0 indicates that there is no relationship between the variables.

The most used measure of correlation is the **Pearson correlation coefficient**, which ranges from -1 to 1. A value of -1 indicates a perfect negative correlation, a value of 0 indicates no correlation, and a value of 1 indicates a perfect positive correlation.

The Pearson correlation coefficient can be used when the relationship of variables is linear and both variables are quantitative and normally distributed. There should be no outliers in the dataset.

Correlation can be calculated using the `cor()` function in R or the `scipy.stats` or `NumPy` libraries in Python.

Probability

Probability is a fundamental concept in machine learning that is used to quantify the uncertainty associated with events or outcomes. Basic concepts of probability include the following:

- **Random variables**: A variable whose value is determined by chance. Random variables can be discrete or continuous.

- **Probability distribution**: A function that describes the likelihood of different values for a random variable. Common probability distributions include the normal distribution, the binomial distribution, and the Poisson distribution.

- **Bayes' theorem**: A fundamental theorem in probability theory that describes the relationship between conditional probabilities. Bayes' theorem is used in many machine-learning algorithms, including naive Bayes classifiers and Bayesian networks.

- **Conditional probability**: The probability of an event occurring given that another event has occurred. Conditional probability is used in many machine-learning algorithms, including decision trees and Markov models.

- **Expected value**: The average value of a random variable, weighted by its probability distribution. Expected value is used in many machine-learning algorithms, including reinforcement learning.

- **Maximum likelihood estimation**: A method of estimating the parameters of a probability distribution based on observed data. Maximum likelihood estimation is used in many machine-learning algorithms, including logistic regression and hidden Markov models.

> **Note**
> Probability is a wide concept on its own and many books have been written about this area. In this book, we are not going deeper into the details but it is important to understand the terms at a high level.

We have now investigated the basic principles of the statistics that play a crucial role in Qlik tools. Next, we will focus on the concept of defining a proper sample size. This is an important step, since we are not always able to train our model with all the data and we want our training dataset to represent the full data as much as possible.

Defining a proper sample size and population

Defining a proper sample size for machine learning is crucial to get accurate results. It is also a common problem that we don't know how much training data is needed. Having a correct sample size is important for several reasons:

- **Generalization:** Machine-learning models are trained on a sample of data with the expectation that they will generalize to new, unseen data. If the sample size is too small, the model may not capture the full complexity of the problem, resulting in poor generalization performance.

- **Overfitting:** Overfitting occurs when a model fits the training data too closely, resulting in poor generalization performance. Overfitting is more likely to occur when the sample size is small because the model has fewer examples to learn from and may be more likely to fit the noise in the data.

- **Statistical significance:** In statistical inference, sample size is an important factor in determining the statistical significance of the results. A larger sample size provides more reliable estimates of model parameters and reduces the likelihood of errors due to random variation.

- **Resource efficiency:** Machine-learning models can be computationally expensive to train, especially with large datasets. Having a correct sample size can help optimize the use of computing resources by reducing the time and computational resources required to train the model.

- **Decision-making:** Machine-learning models are often used to make decisions that have real-world consequences. Having a correct sample size ensures that the model is reliable and trustworthy, reducing the risk of making incorrect or biased decisions based on faulty or inadequate data.

Defining a sample size

The sample size depends on several factors, including the complexity of the problem, the quality of the data, and the algorithm being used. **"How much training data do I need?"** is a common question at the beginning of a machine-learning project. Unfortunately, there is no correct answer to that question, since it depends on various factors. However, there are some guidelines.

Generally, the following factors should be addressed when defining a sample:

- **Have a representative sample**: It is essential to have a representative sample of the population to train a machine-learning model. The sample size should be large enough to capture the variability in the data and ensure that the model is not biased toward a particular subset of the population.

- **Avoid overfitting**: Overfitting occurs when a model is too complex and fits the training data too closely. To avoid overfitting, it is important to have a sufficient sample size to ensure that the model generalizes well to new data.

- **Consider the number of features**: The number of features or variables in the dataset also affects the sample size. As the number of features increases, the sample size required to train the model also increases.

- **Use power analysis**: Power analysis is a statistical technique used to determine the sample size required to detect a significant effect. It can be used to determine the sample size needed for a machine-learning model to achieve a certain level of accuracy or predictive power.

- **Cross-validation**: Cross-validation is a technique used to evaluate the performance of a machine-learning model. It involves splitting the data into training and testing sets and using the testing set to evaluate the model's performance. The sample size should be large enough to ensure that the testing set is representative of the population and provides a reliable estimate of the model's performance.

There are several statistical heuristic methods available to estimate a sample size. Let's take a closer look at some of these.

Power analysis

Power analysis is one of the key concepts in machine learning. Power analysis is mainly used to determine whether a statistical test has sufficient probability to find an effect and to estimate the sample size required for an experiment considering the significance level, effect size, and statistical power.

The definition of a power in this concept is the probability that a statistical test will reject a false null hypothesis ($H0$) or the probability of detecting an effect (depending on whether the effect is there). A bigger sample size will result in a larger power. The main output of power analysis is the estimation of an appropriate sample size.

To understand the basics of power analysis, we need to get familiar with the following concepts:

- A type I error (α) is rejecting a $H0$ or a null hypothesis in the data when it's true (false positive).

- A type II error (β) is the failure to reject a false $H0$ or, in other words, a probability of missing an effect that is in the data (false negative).

- The power is the probability of detecting an effect that is in the data.

- There is a direct relationship between the power and type II error:

  Power = 1 – β

  Generally, β should never be more than 20%, which gives us the minimum approved power level of 80%.

- The significance level (α) is the maximum risk of rejecting a true null hypothesis (*H0*) that you are willing to take. This is typically set to 5% (p < 0.05).

- The effect size is the measure of the strength of a phenomenon in the dataset (independent of sample size). The effect size is typically the hardest to determine. An example of an effect size would be the height difference between men and women. The greater the effect size, the greater the height difference will be. The effect size is typically marked with the letter *d* in formulas.

Now that we have defined the key concepts, let's look how to use power analysis in R and Python to calculate the sample size for an experiment with a simple example. In R we will utilize a package called pwr and with Python we will utilize the NumPy and statsmodels.stats.power libraries.

Let's assume that we would like to create a model of customer behavior. We are interested to know whether there is a difference in the mean price of what our preferred customers and other customers pay at our online shop. How many transactions in each group should we investigate to get the power level of 80%?

R:

```
library(pwr)
ch <- cohen.ES(test = "t", size = "medium")
print(ch)


test <- pwr.t.test(d = 0.5, power = 0.80, sig.level = 0.05)
print(test)
```

The model will give us the following result:

```
     Two-sample t test power calculation

              n = 63.76561
              d = 0.5
      sig.level = 0.05
          power = 0.8
    alternative = two.sided
NOTE: n is number in *each* group
```

So, we will need a sample of 64 transactions in each group.

Python:

```
import numpy as np
from statsmodels.stats.power import TTestIndPower

analysis = TTestIndPower()

sample_size = analysis.solve_power(effect_size = 0.5, alpha = 0.05,
power = 0.8)
print(str(sample_size))
```

Our Python code will produce the same result as our earlier R code, giving us 64 transactions in each group.

> **Note**
>
> Power analysis is a wide and complex topic, but it's important to understand the basics, since it is widely utilized in many machine-learning tools. In this chapter, we have only scratched the surface of this topic.

Sampling

Sampling is a method that makes it possible to get information about the population (dataset) based on the statistics from a subset of population (sample), without having to investigate every individual value. Sampling is particularly useful if a dataset is large and can't be analyzed in full. In this case, identifying and analyzing a representative sample is important. In some cases, a small sample can be enough to reveal the most important information, but generally, using a larger sample can increase the likelihood of representing the data as a whole.

When performing sampling, there are some aspects to consider:

- **Sample goal**: A property that you wish to estimate or predict
- **Population**: A domain from which observations are made
- **Selection criteria**: A method to determine whether an individual value will be accepted as a part of the sample
- **Sample size**: The number of data points that will form the final sample data

Sampling methods can be divided into two main categories:

Probability sampling is a technique where every element of the dataset has an equal chance of being selected. These methods typically give the best chance of creating a sample that truly represents the population. Examples of probability sampling algorithms are *simple random sampling, cluster sampling, systematic sampling,* and *stratified random sampling.*

Non-probability sampling is a method where all elements are not equally qualified for being selected. With these methods, there is a significant risk that the sample is non-representative. Examples of non-probability sampling algorithms are *convenience sampling, selective sampling, snowball sampling,* and *quota sampling.*

When using sampling as a methodology for training set creation, it is recommended to utilize a specialized sampling library in either R or Python. This will automate the process and produce a sample based on selected algorithms and specifications. In R, we can utilize the standard `sample` library and in Python there is a package called `random.sample`. Here is a simple example of random sampling with both languages:

R:

```
dataset <- data.frame(id = 1:20, fact = letters[1:20])
set.seed(123)
sample <- dataset[sample(1:nrow(dataset), size=5), ]
```

The content of the sample frame will look like this:

```
   id fact
15 15   o
19 19   s
14 14   n
3   3   c
10 10   j
```

Python:

```
import random
random.seed(123)
dataset = [[1,'v'],[5,'b'],[7,'f'],[4,'h'],[0,'l']]
sample = random.sample(dataset, 3)
print(sample)
```

The result of the sample vector will look like the following:

```
[[1, 'v'], [7, 'f'], [0, 'l']]
```

> **Note**
>
> There is a lot of material covering different sampling techniques and how to use those with R and Python on the internet. Take some time to practice these techniques with simple datasets.

Sampling errors

In all sampling methods, errors are bound to occur. There are two types of sampling errors:

- **Selection bias** is introduced by the selection of values that are not random to be part of the sample. In this case, the sample is not representative of the dataset that we are looking to analyze.

- **Sampling error** is a statistical error that occurs when we don't select the sample that represents the entire population of data. In this case, the results of the prediction or model will not represent the actual results that are generalized to cover the entire dataset.

Training datasets will always contain a sampling error, since it cannot represent the entire dataset. Sample errors in the context of binary classification can be calculated using the following simplified formula:

$$Sample\ error\ =\ \frac{False\ positive\ +\ False\ negative}{True\ positive\ +\ False\ positive\ +\ True\ negative\ +\ False\ negative}$$

If we have, for example, a dataset containing 45 values and out of these 12 are false values, we will get a sample error of 12/45 = 26.67%.

The above formula can be only utilized in context of binary classification. When estimating the population mean (μ) from a sample mean ($\bar{x}$), the standard error is calculated as follows:

$$SE = \frac{\sigma}{\sqrt{n}}$$

- **SE (Standard Error)**: The standard error is a measure of the variability or uncertainty in a sample statistic. It quantifies how much the sample statistic is expected to vary from the true population parameter. In other words, it gives you an idea of how reliable or precise your sample estimate is.

- **σ (population standard deviation)**: This is the standard deviation of the entire population you're trying to make inferences about. It represents the amount of variability or spread in the population data. In practice, the population standard deviation is often unknown, so you may estimate it using the sample standard deviation (s) when working with sample data.

- **n (sample size)**: The number of observations or data points in your sample.

Example

We are conducting a survey to estimate the average age (mean) of residents in a small town. We collect a random sample of 50 residents and find the following statistics:

- Sample mean ($\bar{x}$): 35 years

- Sample standard deviation (s): 10 years (an estimate of the population standard deviation)

- Sample size (n): 50 residents

  $$SE = \frac{10}{\sqrt{50}} = 1.42 \; years$$

So, the standard error of the sample mean is approximately 1.42 years. This means that if you were to take multiple random samples of the same size from the population and calculate the mean for each sample, you would expect those sample means to vary around 35 years, with an average amount of variation of 1.42 years.

Standard error is often used to construct confidence intervals. For instance, you might use this standard error to calculate a 95% confidence interval for the average age of residents in the town, which would allow you to estimate the range within which the true population mean age is likely to fall with 95% confidence.

As we can see, sample error, often referred to as "sampling error," is not represented by a single formula. Instead, it is a concept that reflects the variability or uncertainty in the estimates or measurements made on a sample of data when trying to infer information about a larger population. The specific formula for sampling error depends on the statistic or parameter you are estimating and the characteristics of your data. In practice, you would use statistical software or tools to calculate the standard error for the specific parameter or estimate you are interested in.

Training and test data in machine learning

The preceding methods for defining a sample size will work well if we need to define the amount of needed data without a large collection of historic data covering the phenomenon that we are investigating. In many cases, we have a large dataset and we would like to produce training and test datasets from that historical data. Training datasets are used to train our machine-learning model and test datasets are used to validate the accuracy of our model. Training and test datasets are the key concepts in machine learning.

We can utilize power analysis and sampling to create training and testing datasets, but sometimes there is no need to make a complex analysis if our sample is already created. The training dataset is the biggest subset of the original dataset and will be used to fit the machine-learning model. The test dataset is another subset of original data and is always independent of the training dataset.

Test data should be well organized and contain data for each type of scenario that the model would be facing in the production environment. Usually it is 20–25% of the total original dataset. An exact split can be adjusted based on the requirements of a problem or the dataset characteristics.

Generating a training and testing dataset from an original dataset can also be done using R or Python. Qlik functions can be used to perform this action in load script.

Now that we have investigated some of the concepts to define a good sample, we can focus on the concepts used to analyze model performance and reliability. These concepts are important, since using these techniques allow us to develop our model further and make sure that it gives proper results.

Concepts to analyze model performance and reliability

Analyzing the performance and reliability of our machine-learning model is an important development step and should be done before implementing the model to production. There are several metrics that you can use to analyze the performance and reliability of a machine learning model, depending on the specific task and problem you are trying to solve. In this section, we will cover some of these techniques, focusing on ones that Qlik tools are using.

Regression model scoring

The following concepts can be used to score and verify **regression models**. Regression models predict outcomes as a number, indicating the model's best estimate of the target variable. We will learn more about regression models in *Chapter 2*.

R^2 (R-squared)

R-squared is a statistical measure that represents the proportion of the variance in a dependent variable that is explained by an independent variable (or variables) in a regression model. In other words, it measures the goodness of fit of a regression model to the data.

R-squared ranges from 0 to 1, where 0 indicates that the model does not explain any of the variability in the dependent variable, and 1 indicates that the model perfectly explains all the variability in the dependent variable.

R-squared is an important measure of the quality of a regression model. A high R-squared value indicates that the model fits the data well and that the independent variable(s) have a strong relationship with the dependent variable. A low R-squared value indicates that the model does not fit the data well and that the independent variable(s) do not have a strong relationship with the dependent variable. However, it is important to note that a high R-squared value does not necessarily mean that the model is the best possible model, so other factors such as overfitting should also be taken into consideration when evaluating the performance of a model. R-squared is often used together with other metrics and it should be interpreted in the context of the problem. The formula for R-squared is the following:

$$R^2 = \frac{Variance\ explained\ by\ the\ model}{Total\ variance}$$

There are some limitations for R-squared. It cannot be used to check whether the prediction is biased or not and it doesn't tell us whether the regression model has an adequate fit or not. Bias refers to systematic errors in predictions. To check for bias, you should analyze residuals (differences between predicted and observed values) or use bias-specific metrics such as **Mean Absolute Error** (MAE) and **Mean Bias Deviation** (MBD). R-squared primarily addresses model variance, not bias.

Sometimes it is better to utilize **adjusted R-squared**. Adjusted R-squared is a modified version of the standard R-squared used in regression analysis. We can use adjusted R-squared when dealing with multiple predictors to assess model fit, control overfitting, compare models with different predictors, and aid in feature selection. It accounts for the number of predictors, penalizing unnecessary complexity. However, it should be used alongside other evaluation metrics and domain knowledge for a comprehensive model assessment.

Root mean squared error (RMSE), mean absolute error (MAE), and mean squared error (MSE)

Root mean squared error is the average difference that can be expected between predicted and actual value. It is the standard deviation of the **residuals** (prediction errors) and tells us how concentrated the data is around the "line of best fit." It is a standard way to measure the error of a model when predicting quantitative data. RMSE is always measured in the same unit as the target value.

As an example of RMSE, if we have a model that predicts house value in a certain area and we get an RMSE of 20,000, it means that, on average, the predicted value differs 20,000 USD from the actual value.

Mean absolute error is defined as an average of all absolute prediction errors in all data points. In MAE, different errors are not weighted but the scores increase linearly with the increase in error. MAE is always a positive value since we are using an absolute value of error. MAE is useful when the errors are symmetrically distributed and there are no significant outliers.

Mean squared error is a squared average difference between the predicted and actual value. Squaring eliminates the negative values and ensures that MSE is always positive or 0. The smaller the MSE, the closer our model to the "line of best fit." RMSE can be calculated using MSE. RMSE is a square root of MSE.

When to use the above metrics in practice

MAE is robust to outliers and provides a straightforward interpretation of the average error magnitude.

MSE penalizes large errors more heavily and is suitable when you want to minimize the impact of outliers on the error metric.

RMSE is similar to MSE but provides a more interpretable error metric in the same units as the target variable.

The choice between these metrics should align with your specific problem and objectives. Its also good practice to consider the nature of your data and the impact of outliers when selecting an error metric. Additionally, you can use these metrics in conjunction with other evaluation techniques to get a comprehensive view of your model's performance.

Multiclass classification scoring and binary classification scoring

The following concepts can be used to score and verify multiclass and binary models. Binary classification models distribute outcomes into two categories, typically denoted as Yes or No. Multiclass classification models are similar, but there are more than two categories as an outcome. We will learn more about both models in *Chapter 2*.

Recall

Recall measures the percentage of correctly classified positive instances over the total number of actual positive instances. In other words, recall represents the ability of a model to correctly capture all positive instances.

Recall is calculated as follows:

$$Recall = \frac{True\ positive}{(True\ positive + False\ negative)}$$

A high recall indicates that the model is able to accurately capture all positive instances and has a low rate of false negatives. On the other hand, a low recall indicates that the model is missing many positive instances, resulting in a high rate of false negatives.

Precision

Precision measures the percentage of correctly classified positive instances over the total number of predicted positive instances. In other words, precision represents the ability of the model to correctly identify positive instances.

Precision is calculated as follows:

$$Precision = \frac{True\ positive}{(True\ positive + False\ positive)}$$

A high precision indicates that the model is able to accurately identify positive instances and has a low rate of false positives. On the other hand, a low precision indicates that the model is incorrectly classifying many instances as positive, resulting in a high rate of false positives.

Precision is particularly useful in situations where false positives are costly or undesirable, such as in medical diagnosis or fraud detection. Precision should be used in conjunction with other metrics, such as **recall** and **F1 score**, to get a more complete picture of the model's performance.

F1 score

The F1 score is defined as the harmonic mean of precision and recall, and it ranges from 0 to 1, with higher values indicating better performance. The formula for F1 score is as follows:

$$F1\ score = 2 * \frac{(precision * recall)}{(precision + recall)}$$

The F1 score gives equal importance to both precision and recall, making it a useful metric for evaluating models when the distribution of positive and negative instances is uneven. A high F1 score indicates that the model has a good balance between precision and recall and can accurately classify both positive and negative instances.

In general, the more imbalanced the dataset is, the lower the F1 score is likely to be. It's crucial to recognize that, when dealing with highly imbalanced datasets where one class greatly outnumbers the other, the F1 score may be influenced. A more imbalanced dataset can result in a reduced F1 score. Being aware of this connection can assist in interpreting F1 scores within the context of particular data distributions and problem domains. If the F1 value is high, all other metrics will be high as well, and if it is low, there is a need for further analysis.

Accuracy

Accuracy measures the percentage of correctly classified instances over the total number of instances. In other words, accuracy represents the ability of the model to correctly classify both positive and negative instances.

Accuracy is calculated in the following way:

$$Accuracy = \frac{(True\ positive + True\ negative)}{(True\ positive + False\ positive + True\ negative + False\ negative)}$$

A high accuracy indicates that the model is able to accurately classify both positive and negative instances and has a low rate of false positives and false negatives. However, accuracy can be misleading in situations where the distribution of positive and negative instances is uneven. In such cases, other metrics such as precision, recall, and F1 score may provide a more accurate representation of the model's performance.

Accuracy can mislead in imbalanced datasets where one class vastly outnumbers the others. This is because accuracy doesn't consider the class distribution and can be high even if the model predicts the majority class exclusively. To address this, use metrics such as precision, recall, F1-score, **AUC-ROC**, and **AUC-PR**, which provide a more accurate evaluation of model performance by focusing on the correct identification of the minority class, which is often the class of interest in such datasets.

Example scenario

Suppose we are developing a machine-learning model to detect a rare disease that occurs in only 1% of the population. We collect a dataset of 10,000 patient records:

- 100 patients have the rare disease (positive class)
- 9,900 patients do not have the disease (negative class)

Now, let's say our model predicts all 10,000 patients as not having the disease. Here's what happens:

- True Positives (correctly predicted patients with the disease): 0

- False Positives (incorrectly predicted patients with the disease): 0

- True Negatives (correctly predicted patients without the disease): 9,900

- False Negatives (incorrectly predicted patients without the disease): 100

Using accuracy as our evaluation metric produces the following result:

$$Accuracy = \frac{True\ positive + True\ negative}{Total} = \frac{9900}{10000} = 99\%$$

Our model appears to have an impressive 99% accuracy, which might lead to the misleading conclusion that it's performing exceptionally well. However, it has completely failed to detect any cases of the rare disease (True Positives = 0), which is the most critical aspect of the problem.

In this example, accuracy doesn't provide an accurate picture of the model's performance because it doesn't account for the severe class imbalance and the importance of correctly identifying the minority class (patients with the disease).

Confusion matrix

A confusion matrix is a table used to evaluate the performance of a classification model. It displays the number of true positive, false positive, true negative, and false negative predictions made by the model for a set of test data.

The four elements in the confusion matrix represent the following:

- True positives (TP) are actual true values that were correctly predicted as true

- False positives (FP) are actual false values that were incorrectly predicted as true

- False negatives (FN) are actual true values that were incorrectly predicted as false

- True negatives (TN) are actual false values that were correctly predicted as false

Qlik AutoML presents a confusion matrix as part of the experiment view. Below the numbers in each quadrant, you can also see percentage values for the metrics recall (TP), fallout (FP), miss rate (FN), and specificity (TN).

An example of the confusion matrix of Qlik AutoML can be seen in the following figure:

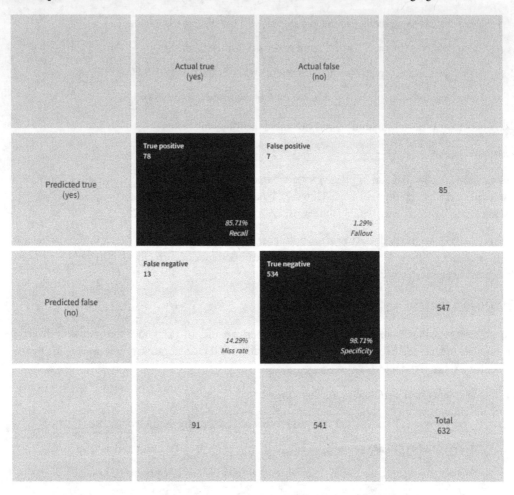

Figure 1.4: Confusion matrix as seen in Qlik AutoML

By analyzing the confusion matrix, we can calculate various performance metrics such as accuracy, precision, recall, and F1 score, which can help us understand how well the model is performing on the test data. The confusion matrix can also help us identify any patterns or biases in the model's predictions and adjust the model accordingly.

Matthews Correlation Coefficient (MCC)

The Matthews Correlation Coefficient metric can be used to evaluate the performance of a binary classification model, particularly when dealing with imbalanced data.

MCC takes into account all four elements of the confusion matrix (true positives, false positives, true negatives, and false negatives) to provide a measure of the quality of a binary classifier's predictions. It ranges between -1 and +1, with a value of +1 indicating perfect classification performance, 0 indicating a random classification, and -1 indicating complete disagreement between predicted and actual values.

The formula for MCC is as follows:

$$MCC = \frac{(TP \times TN - FP \times FN)}{\sqrt{((TP + FP) \times (TP + FN) \times (TN + FP) \times (TN + FN))}}$$

MCC is particularly useful when dealing with imbalanced datasets where the number of positive and negative instances is not equal. It provides a better measure of classification performance than accuracy in such cases, since accuracy can be biased toward the majority class.

AUC and ROC curve

The ROC (Receiver Operating Characteristic) curve is a graphical representation of the performance of a binary classification model that allows us to evaluate and compare different models based on their ability to discriminate between positive and negative classes. AUC describes the area under the curve.

An ROC curve plots the **True Positive Rate (TPR)** against the **False Positive Rate (FPR)** at various classification thresholds. The TPR is the ratio of true positive predictions to the total number of actual positive instances, while the FPR is the ratio of false positive predictions to the total number of actual negative instances.

By varying the classification threshold, we can obtain different TPR and FPR pairs and plot them on the ROC curve. The area under the ROC curve (AUC-ROC) is used as a performance metric for binary classification models, with higher AUC-ROC indicating better performance.

A perfect classifier would have an AUC-ROC of 1.0, indicating that it has a high TPR and low FPR across all possible classification thresholds. A random classifier would have an AUC-ROC of 0.5, indicating that its TPR and FPR are equal and its performance is no better than chance.

The ROC curve and AUC-ROC are useful for evaluating and comparing binary classification models, especially when the positive and negative classes are imbalanced or when the cost of false positive and false negative errors is different.

The following figure represents an ROC curve as seen in Qlik AutoML. The figure shows a pretty good ROC curve (it is good since the curve should be as close to 1 as possible). The dotted line is 50:50 random chance.

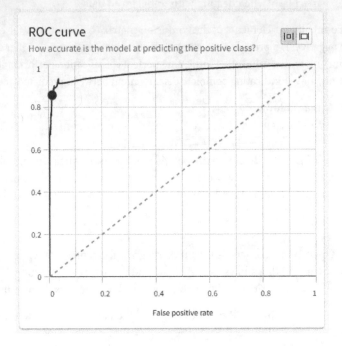

Figure 1.5: ROC curve for a good model in Qlik AutoML

Threshold

In binary classification, a **threshold** is a value that is used to decide whether an instance should be classified as positive or negative by a model.

When a model makes a prediction, it generates a probability score between 0 and 1 that represents the likelihood of an instance belonging to the positive class. If the score is above a certain threshold value, the instance is classified as positive, and if it is below the threshold, it is classified as negative.

The choice of threshold can significantly impact the performance of a classification model. If the threshold is set too high, the model may miss many positive instances, leading to a low recall and high precision. Conversely, if the threshold is set too low, the model may classify many negative instances as positive, leading to a high recall and low precision.

Therefore, selecting an appropriate threshold for a classification model is important in achieving the desired balance between precision and recall. The optimal threshold depends on the specific application and the cost of false positive and false negative errors.

Qlik AutoML computes the precision and recall for hundreds of possible threshold values from 0 to 1. A threshold achieving the highest F1 score is chosen. By selecting a threshold, the produced predictions are more robust for imbalanced datasets.

Feature importance

Feature importance is a measure of the contribution of each input variable (feature) in a model to the output variable (prediction). It is a way to understand which features have the most impact on the model's prediction, and which features can be ignored or removed without significantly affecting the model's performance.

Feature importance can be computed using various methods, depending on the type of model used. Some common methods for calculating feature importance include the following:

- **Permutation importance:** This method involves shuffling the values of each feature in the test data, one at a time, and measuring the impact on the model's performance. The features that cause the largest drop in performance when shuffled are considered more important.

- **Feature importance from tree-based models:** In decision tree-based models such as Random Forest or Gradient Boosting, feature importance can be calculated based on how much each feature decreases the impurity of the tree. The features that reduce impurity the most are considered more important.

- **Coefficient magnitude:** In linear models such as Linear Regression or Logistic Regression, feature importance can be calculated based on the magnitude of the coefficients assigned to each feature. The features with larger coefficients are considered more important.

Feature importance can help in understanding the relationship between the input variables and the model's prediction and can guide feature selection and engineering efforts to improve the model's performance. It can also provide insights into the underlying problem and the data being used and can help in identifying potential biases or data quality issues.

In Qlik AutoML, the permutation importance of each feature is represented as a graph. This can be used to estimate feature importance. Another method that is visible in AutoML is SHAP importance values. The next section will cover the principles of SHAP importance values.

SHAP values

SHAP (SHapley Additive exPlanations) values are a technique for interpreting the output of machine-learning models by assigning an importance score to each input feature.

SHAP values are based on game theory and the concept of Shapley values, which provide a way to fairly distribute the value of a cooperative game among its players. In the context of machine learning, the game is the prediction task, and the players are the input features. The SHAP values represent the contribution of each feature to the difference between a specific prediction and the expected value of the output variable.

The SHAP values approach involves computing the contribution of each feature by evaluating the model's output for all possible combinations of features, with and without the feature of interest. The contribution of the feature is the difference in the model's output between the two cases averaged over all possible combinations.

SHAP values provide a more nuanced understanding of the relationship between the input features and the model's output than other feature importance measures, as they account for interactions between features and the potential correlation between them.

SHAP values can be visualized using a SHAP plot, which shows the contribution of each feature to the model's output for a specific prediction. This plot can help in understanding the relative importance of each feature and how they are influencing the model's prediction.

Difference between SHAP and permutation importance

Permutation importance and SHAP are alternative ways of measuring feature importance. The main difference between the two is that permutation importance is based on the decrease in model performance. It is a simpler and more computationally efficient approach to compute feature importance but may not accurately reflect the true importance of features in complex models.

SHAP importance is based on the magnitude of feature attributions. SHAP values provide a more nuanced understanding of feature importance but can be computationally expensive and may not be feasible for very large datasets or complex models.

Permutation importance can be used to do the following:

- Understand which features to keep and which to abandon
- Understand the feature importance for model accuracy
- Understand if there is a data leakage, meaning information from outside the training dataset is used to create or evaluate a model, resulting in over-optimistic performance estimates or incorrect predictions

SHAP importance can be used to do the following:

- Understand which features have greatest influence to the predicted outcome
- Understand how the different values of the feature affect the model prediction
- Understand what the most influential rows are in the dataset

We can see an example of a permutation importance graph and SHAP graph in the following figure, as seen in Qlik AutoML:

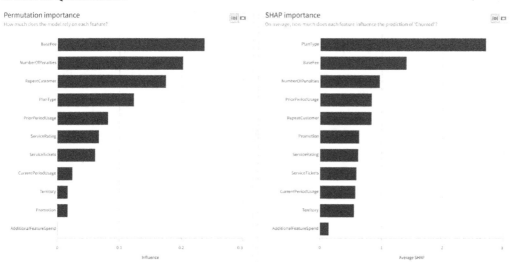

Figure 1.6: Permutation importance and SHAP importance graphs

> **Note**
>
> We will utilize both permutation importance and SHAP importance in our hands-on examples later in this book.

Summary

In this chapter, we first got an introduction of Qlik tools for machine learning. We discovered the key features of the platform and how different components can be utilized. Understanding the key components is important since we will be utilizing Insight Advisor, AutoML, and Advanced Analytics Integration later in this book.

We also discovered some of the key concepts of statistics. Understanding the basics of the underlying mathematics is crucial to understanding the models. We only scratched the surface of the mathematics, but this should be enough to familiarize you with the terminology. We also touched on the important topic of sample and sample size. When creating a model, we need to train it with training data. Determining a reasonable sample size will help us to get an accurate model without wasting resources.

At the end of this chapter, we got familiar with some of the techniques to validate the model's performance and reliability. These are important concepts, since Qlik tools are using the introduced methods to communicate the metrics of the model.

In the next chapter, we will augment our background knowledge by getting familiar with some of the most common machine-learning algorithms. These algorithms will be used in later parts of this book.

2

Machine Learning Algorithms and Models with Qlik

Machine learning algorithms have become an integral part of our lives, from the personalization of online ads to the recommendation systems on streaming platforms. These algorithms are responsible for making intelligent decisions based on data, without being explicitly programmed.

Machine learning algorithms refer to a set of mathematical models and techniques that enable software to learn patterns and relationships from data, allowing them to make predictions and decisions. These algorithms can be broadly categorized into supervised, unsupervised, semi-supervised, and reinforcement learning algorithms. Each type of algorithm has its own unique characteristics and applications, suiting them to a wide range of tasks.

In this chapter, we will provide an overview of machine learning algorithms and their applications, focusing on algorithms used in Qlik tools. Here is what you will learn as a part of this chapter:

- Understand regression models and how to use these

- Understand different clustering algorithms and decision trees

- Understand the basics of boosting algorithms, especially the one used in Qlik AutoML

- Understand the basics of neural networks and other advanced machine learning models

> **Note**
>
> Qlik AutoML was using the following algorithms at the time of writing this book:
>
> **Binary and multiclass classification problems:**
>
> CatBoost Classification, Elastic Net Regression, Gaussian Naive Bayes, Lasso Regression, LightGBM Classification, Logistic Regression, Random Forest Classification, XGBoost Classification
>
> **Regression problems:**
>
> CatBoost Regression, LightGBM Regression, Linear Regression, Random Forest Regression, SGD Regression, XGBoost Regression
>
> Some of these algorithms will be covered in more detail in the coming sections.

Regression models

Regression models are a type of supervised machine-learning model used to predict continuous numerical values for a target variable based on one or more input variables. In other words, regression models are used to estimate the relationships between the input variables and the output variable.

There are various types of regression models used in machine learning, some of which include the following:

- **Linear Regression**: This is a type of regression model that assumes a linear relationship between the input variables and the output variable.

- **Polynomial Regression**: This is a type of regression model that assumes a polynomial relationship between the input variables and the output variable.

- **Logistic Regression**: This is a type of regression model used to predict binary or categorical outcomes. It estimates the probability of an event occurring based on the input variables.

- **Ridge Regression**: This is a type of linear regression model that uses regularization to prevent overfitting of the model.

- **Lasso Regression**: This is another type of linear regression model that uses regularization to prevent overfitting of the model. It is particularly useful when dealing with datasets that have a large number of features.

In the next section, we are going to take a closer look at some of the regression models in the preceding list.

Linear regression

Linear regression is used for modeling the relationship between a dependent variable (also known as the target or response variable) and one or more independent variables (also known as the explanatory or predictor variables). The goal of linear regression is to find the best-fit line (or hyperplane) that can predict the dependent variable based on the values of the independent variables. In other words, linear regression tries to find a linear equation that relates the input variables to the output variable. The equation takes the following form:

$Y = mX + b + e$

where Y is the dependent variable, X is the independent variable, m is the slope of the line, b is the intercept, and e represents the error of the model. The goal of linear regression is to find the best values of m and b that minimize the difference between the predicted values and the actual values of the dependent variable. In simple linear regression, we have one independent variable and in multiple linear regression, we will have multiple independent variables.

Example

We want to investigate the relationship between the number of hours a student studies and their exam score. We collect data from 10 students, recording the number of hours they studied and their corresponding exam scores. The data is shown here:

Hours studied (X)	Exam score (Y)
2	60
3	70
4	80
5	85
6	90
7	95
8	100
9	105
10	110
11	115

Table 2.1: Exam score data

We can use a simple linear regression model to model the relationship between the two variables, with the number of hours studied as the independent variable (X) and the exam score as the dependent variable (Y). The model takes the following form:

$Y = mX + b + e$

where b is the intercept (the value of Y when $X=0$) and m is the slope (the rate at which Y changes with respect to X). To estimate the values of b and m, we can use the least squares method. Solving for the regression equation, we get the following:

$$Y = 5*X + 55 + e$$

This equation tells us that, on average, for every additional hour studied, a student can expect to score 5 points higher on the exam. The intercept of 55 tells us that a student who studies 0 hours can expect to score 55 points (which may not be realistic, but it's just the mathematical extrapolation from the model).

We can use this model to make predictions about exam scores based on the number of hours studied. For example, if a student studies for 7 hours, we can estimate their exam score to be as follows:

$$Y = 5*7 + 55 + e = 90 + e$$

Logistic regression

Logistic regression is a statistical method used for binary classification problems where the outcome variable is categorical and has only two possible values, such as "yes" or "no," "pass" or "fail," or "spam" or "not spam." It is a type of regression analysis that models the relationship between the independent variables and the dependent variable by estimating the probability of the binary outcome.

The logistic regression model uses a logistic function, also known as the sigmoid function, to model the relationship between the input variables and the binary outcome. The sigmoid function transforms the input values into a range between 0 and 1, which represents the probability of the binary outcome.

The logistic regression model can be trained using a maximum likelihood estimation method to find the parameters that maximize the likelihood of the observed data given the model. These parameters can then be used to predict the probability of the binary outcome for new input data.

Logistic regression is widely used in medical diagnosis, credit scoring, and marketing analysis. It is a popular algorithm due to its simplicity and interpretability.

Example

Let's say we want to predict whether or not a customer will purchase a product based on their age and income. We have a dataset of 90 customers, where each row represents a customer and the columns represent their age, income, and whether or not they purchased the product (0 for not purchased, 1 for purchased).

We can use logistic regression to model the probability of a customer purchasing the product based on their age and income. The logistic regression model can be expressed as the following:

$$p(purchase) = \frac{1}{(1 + exp(-(\beta 0 + \beta 1 * age + \beta 2 * income)))}$$

where $\beta 0$, $\beta 1$, and $\beta 2$ are the parameters of the model that we need to estimate from the data.

We can estimate these parameters using maximum likelihood estimation. Once we have estimated the parameters, we can use the model to predict the probability of a customer purchasing the product for new customers based on their age and income.

For example, if a new customer is 35 years old and has an income of $50,000, we can use the model to predict their probability of purchasing the product as follows:

$$p(purchase) = \frac{1}{(1 + exp(-(\beta 0 + \beta 1 * 35 + \beta 2 * 50000)))}$$

We can then use a decision threshold, such as 0.5, to determine whether to classify the customer as a purchaser or non-purchaser. Note that a choice of threshold can affect the trade-off between precision and recall.

We can solve the above problem with R and Python using the corresponding libraries. Let's take a look at how to do that. In the following examples, we are going to use a sample dataset called customer_data.csv.

Here is an overview of the datafile:

Age	Income	purchased
22	20000	0
35	80000	1
42	50000	0
27	30000	0
48	70000	1
38	60000	1
41	45000	0
29	35000	0
33	40000	1

Table 2.2: Customer data

Example solution with R

The following code reads customer data from a CSV file, builds a logistic regression model to predict the probability of a customer making a purchase based on their age and income, and then predicts the probability for a new customer and provides a corresponding prediction message based on the probability value:

```
data <- read.csv('customer_data.csv')
model <- glm(purchased ~ age + income, data = data, family =
binomial())
new_customer <- data.frame(age = 35, income = 50000)
```

```
prob_purchase <- predict(model, new_customer, type = "response")
if (prob_purchase >= 0.5) {
  print("The customer is predicted to purchase the product.")
} else {
  print("The customer is predicted not to purchase the product.")
}
```

Example solution with Python

This code reads customer data from a CSV file into a pandas DataFrame, uses scikit-learn's `LogisticRegression` class to build a logistic regression model to predict purchase probabilities based on age and income, and then predicts the probability for a new customer and provides a corresponding prediction message based on the probability value:

```
import pandas as pd
data = pd.read_csv("customer_data.csv")
from sklearn.linear_model import LogisticRegression
model = LogisticRegression()
model.fit(data[['age', 'income']], data['purchased'])
new_customer = pd.DataFrame({'age': [35], 'income': [50000]})
prob_purchase = model.predict_proba(new_customer)[:, 1]
if prob_purchase >= 0.5:
    print("The customer is predicted to purchase the product.")
else:
    print("The customer is predicted not to purchase the product.")
```

The example will print "**The customer is predicted to purchase the product**" with a probability of 0.81.

Lasso regression

Lasso regression or least absolute shrinkage and selection operator (also known as L1 regularization) is a type of linear regression method used for variable selection and regularization. It is a regression technique that adds a penalty term to the sum of squared errors, which includes the absolute values of the regression coefficients.

The lasso regression algorithm aims to minimize the residual sum of squares subject to the constraint that the sum of absolute values of the coefficients is less than or equal to a constant value. This constraint causes some coefficients to be shrunk toward zero, resulting in sparse models, whereas some features have zero coefficients, effectively excluding them from the model.

Lasso regression is particularly useful when dealing with high-dimensional datasets, where the number of features (or predictors) is much larger than the number of observations. It can also help to overcome problems such as overfitting in linear regression models, where the model becomes too complex and fits the training data too well but fails to generalize well to new data.

Example

We have a dataset that contains information about houses and their sale prices, including features such as the number of bedrooms, the size of the lot, the age of the house, and the location. We want to build a model that can predict the sale price of a house based on these features.

To build this model, we can use Lasso regression. We start by splitting our dataset into a training set and a test set. We then use the training set to fit a Lasso regression model with a specific value of the regularization parameter (alpha). We can tune this parameter using cross-validation to find the best value that results in the lowest error on the test set.

Once we have trained our model, we can use it to make predictions on new data by inputting the values of the features and computing the corresponding sale price. The Lasso regression model will automatically select the most important features for prediction by shrinking the coefficients of less important features toward zero.

For example, let's say our Lasso regression model selected the number of bedrooms and the location as the most important features for predicting the sale price and shrunk the coefficients of the other features to zero. We can use this information to inform our decision-making when buying or selling houses.

Let's take a look at how a sample solution would work in both R and Python. Both examples use the California Housing dataset, split the data into training and testing sets, fit a Lasso regression model, predict on the test set, and evaluate the model's performance on the testing set using the RMSE metric.

Example solution with R

The code performs a linear regression using the Lasso regularization (L1 penalty) to predict the median house values based on a housing dataset. The dataset is loaded from a specific URL, and after preprocessing, it is split into training and testing sets. The glmnet library is used to build the model, and the **Root Mean Squared Error** (**RMSE**) is calculated to evaluate the model's performance:

```
url <- "https://raw.githubusercontent.com/ageron/handson-ml2/master/
datasets/housing/housing.csv"
housing <- read.csv(url)
housing <- na.omit(housing)
set.seed(123)
train_index <- sample(nrow(housing), nrow(housing) * 0.8)
train <- housing[train_index, ]
test <- housing[-train_index, ]
library(glmnet)
x <- model.matrix(median_house_value ~ ., train)[,-1]
y <- train$median_house_value
model <- cv.glmnet(x, y, alpha = 1)
x_test <- model.matrix(median_house_value ~ ., test)[,-1]
y_test <- test$median_house_value
predictions <- predict(model, newx = x_test)
```

```
rmse <- sqrt(mean((predictions - y_test)^2))
print(paste0("RMSE: ", rmse))
```

Example solution with Python

The following code begins by importing pandas and assigning it the alias `pd` for convenience. Next, it reads data from a CSV file hosted at a specific URL and creates a DataFrame named "housing" to hold the dataset. To handle categorical data effectively, the code performs one-hot encoding on the `ocean_proximity` column, converting it into multiple binary columns.

Data cleanliness is vital for reliable models, so the script takes care of missing values by removing any rows containing NaN entries from the DataFrame. The dataset is then split into training and testing sets using the `train_test_split` function from scikit-learn, where 80% of the data is used for training and the remaining 20% for testing.

Now comes the machine-learning part. The script imports the `LassoCV` class from scikit-learn, which is a linear regression model with L1 regularization (Lasso). `LassoCV` performs cross-validation to find the optimal regularization strength (alpha) from a predefined set of values. The model is then trained on the training data using the "`fit`" method.

After training, the model is put to the test. Predictions are made on the testing data using the trained `LassoCV` model, and the performance of the model is assessed using the RMSE metric. The RMSE represents the deviation between the predicted `median_house_value` and the actual target values in the testing data. A lower RMSE indicates better predictive accuracy.

Finally, the script concludes by displaying the calculated RMSE value, providing insight into how well the `LassoCV` model performs in predicting `median_house_value` on unseen data:

```
import pandas as pd
url = "https://raw.githubusercontent.com/ageron/handson-ml2/master/
datasets/housing/housing.csv"
housing = pd.read_csv(url)
housing = pd.get_dummies(housing, columns=['ocean_proximity'])
housing.dropna(inplace=True)
from sklearn.model_selection import train_test_split
X_train, X_test, y_train, y_test = train_test_split(housing.
drop(columns=['median_house_value']), housing['median_house_value'],
test_size=0.2, random_state=123)
from sklearn.linear_model import LassoCV
model = LassoCV(alphas=[0.001, 0.01, 0.1, 1], cv=5)
model.fit(X_train, y_train)
from sklearn.metrics import mean_squared_error
predictions = model.predict(X_test)
rmse = mean_squared_error(y_test, predictions, squared=False)
print(f"RMSE: {rmse}")
```

In the Python example, we have to one-hot encode the `ocean_proximity` feature before splitting the data into training and testing sets, which will allow the Lasso regression model to use the feature in the model. Both models will give us predictions and print RMSE of around 67,000 to 68,000 depending on the version of the libraries used.

> **Note**
>
> In this section, we took a closer look at Lasso regression (L1 regularization). L2 regularization is used with Ridge regression. Lasso and Ridge regression differ mainly in the type of regularization they apply, their impact on feature selection, and their handling of multicollinearity. Lasso tends to produce sparse models with feature selection, while Ridge maintains all features but with smaller coefficients, making it more suitable when multicollinearity is a concern or if you want to control the magnitude of coefficients. The choice between them depends on your specific modeling goals and the nature of your data. We are not going to dive into the details of Ridge regression in this chapter.

In this chapter, we have investigated various linear regression models and how to implement these using R and Python. Linear regression models are an essential part of machine learning and understanding the principles is an important skill. In the next section, we will take a closer look into clustering algorithms, decision trees, and random forests.

Clustering algorithms, decision trees, and random forests

Clustering algorithms are used for unsupervised learning tasks, which means they are used to find patterns in data without any predefined labels or categories. The goal of clustering algorithms is to group similar data points together in clusters, while keeping dissimilar data points separate.

There are several types of clustering algorithms, including K-means, hierarchical clustering, and density-based clustering. K-means is a popular clustering algorithm that works by dividing a dataset into K clusters, where K is a predefined number of clusters. Hierarchical clustering is another clustering algorithm that creates a hierarchy of clusters based on the similarity between data points. Density-based clustering algorithms, such as DBSCAN, group together data points that are closely packed together in high-density regions.

Decision trees, on the other hand, are used for supervised learning tasks, which means they are used to make predictions or decisions based on input data with predefined labels or categories. A decision tree is a tree-like structure that consists of nodes and branches, where each node represents a feature or attribute, and each branch represents a decision based on that feature. The goal of a decision tree is to create a model that can accurately predict the label or category of a new input based on its features.

There are several types of decision trees, including ID3, C4.5, and CART. The ID3 algorithm is a popular decision tree algorithm that works by choosing the attribute with the highest information gain as the root node, and recursively building the tree by selecting attributes that maximize information gain at each level. The C4.5 algorithm is an improved version of ID3 that can handle continuous and discrete data, and CART is another decision tree algorithm that can handle both classification and regression tasks.

Random forests combine multiple decision trees to create a more accurate and robust model. A random forest consists of a large number of decision trees, each trained on a different subset of the data and using a random subset of the available features. This helps to reduce overfitting and increase the generalization ability of the model.

The random subset of features used for each tree is selected randomly from the available features, with a new subset selected for each tree. This ensures that each tree in the forest is different and provides a diverse set of predictions. During training, each tree in the forest is grown to its full depth, and predictions are made by aggregating the predictions of all the trees in the forest.

The aggregation process can vary depending on the task at hand. For classification tasks, the most common method is to use a majority vote, where the final prediction is the class that is predicted by the most trees in the forest. For regression tasks, the most common method is to use the average prediction of all the trees in the forest.

Random forests have several advantages over a single decision tree, including improved accuracy, reduced overfitting, and robustness to noise and outliers in the data. They are also relatively easy to use and can handle a wide range of input features and data types. However, they can be computationally expensive to train and can be difficult to interpret and visualize, especially when dealing with a large number of trees.

In the next sections, we will take a closer look at some of the clustering and decision tree algorithms.

K-means clustering

K-means clustering is a popular algorithm used to partition a set of data points into K clusters, where K is a predefined number. The algorithm works by iteratively assigning data points to the nearest cluster centroid and updating the cluster centroids based on the new assignments.

Here's a simple step-by-step overview of how the K-means algorithm works:

1. Initialize K centroids randomly from the data points.
2. Assign each data point to the nearest centroid based on the Euclidean distance between the data point and the centroid.

3. Update the centroids of each cluster by computing the mean of all the data points assigned to that cluster.

4. Repeat steps 2 and 3 until the centroids no longer move significantly or a maximum number of iterations is reached.

The goal of the K-means algorithm is to minimize the sum of squared distances between each data point and its assigned cluster centroid, also known as the "inertia." The algorithm can be sensitive to the initial random selection of centroids, so it's often a good idea to run the algorithm multiple times with different initializations and select the solution with the lowest inertia.

K-means is a fast and effective algorithm for clustering data, but it does have some limitations. It assumes that the clusters are spherical and of equal size, and it can be sensitive to outliers and noise in the data. Additionally, determining the optimal number of clusters, K, can be challenging and may require some domain knowledge or trial and error.

Example

The iris dataset contains measurements of four features (sepal length, sepal width, petal length, and petal width) for 150 iris flowers, with 50 flowers from each of three species (setosa, versicolor, and virginica). We can use K-means clustering to group these flowers into distinct clusters based on their feature values.

To do this, we first select the features we want to cluster on and preprocess the data by scaling the features to have zero mean and unit variance. Scaling is done to ensure that we have equal influence of features. We then apply the K-means algorithm to the preprocessed data, specifying the number of clusters K we want to create. In this case, we might choose K=3 to correspond to the three iris species.

The K-means algorithm then partitions the flowers into K clusters based on their feature values, with each cluster represented by its centroid (the mean feature values of the flowers assigned to the cluster). We can examine the resulting clusters and their centroids to gain insights into the structure of the iris dataset.

For example, we might find that one cluster contains flowers with smaller sepal and petal dimensions, which could correspond to the setosa species. Another cluster might contain flowers with larger petal dimensions and intermediate sepal dimensions, which could correspond to the versicolor species. The third cluster might contain flowers with larger sepal dimensions and larger petal dimensions, which could correspond to the virginica species.

By using K-means clustering to group the iris flowers based on their feature values, we can gain a deeper understanding of the structure of the dataset and potentially identify patterns and relationships in data. Let's see how the above example would look in R and Python.

Example with R

The following R code uses the "iris" dataset, a popular dataset in the machine-learning community. It performs K-means clustering on the dataset's four numeric attributes: Sepal.Length, Sepal.Width, Petal.Length, and Petal.Width. The code sets a random seed for reproducibility and applies the K-means algorithm with three cluster centers. After the clustering is performed, the code displays the cluster assignments for each data point, indicating which cluster each observation belongs to (represented by values 1, 2, or 3). K-means clustering aims to group similar data points into clusters and is a common technique for unsupervised machine learning tasks:

```
data(iris)
iris_cluster <- iris[, c("Sepal.Length", "Sepal.Width", "Petal.
Length", "Petal.Width")]
set.seed(123)
kmeans_results <- kmeans(iris_cluster, centers = 3)
kmeans_results$cluster
```

Example with Python

The following Python code uses the scikit-learn library to perform K-means clustering on the Iris dataset. The Iris dataset is loaded using load_iris() from scikit-learn, containing measurements of iris flowers' sepal length, sepal width, petal length, and petal width, along with their corresponding species labels.

The script extracts the four feature columns for clustering and stores them in the iris_cluster variable. Then, it imports the KMeans class from scikit-learn's sklearn.cluster module.

The K-means algorithm is applied to the feature data (iris_cluster) with the number of clusters (n_clusters) set to 3. The random_state parameter is set to 123 to ensure the reproducibility of the results.

After clustering, the code prints the cluster assignments for each data point in the Iris dataset. Each data point is assigned a cluster label (0, 1, or 2), indicating the group it belongs to according to the K-means clustering:

```
from sklearn.datasets import load_iris
iris = load_iris()
iris_cluster = iris.data[:, [0, 1, 2, 3]]
from sklearn.cluster import KMeans
kmeans_results = KMeans(n_clusters=3, random_state=123).fit(iris_
cluster)
print(kmeans_results.labels_)
```

Both of the code examples will print the cluster assignments for the iris dataset. The result looks similar to the following:

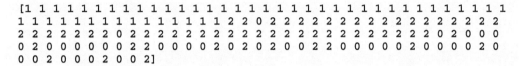

```
[1 1 1 1 1 1 1 1 1 1 1 1 1 1 1 1 1 1 1 1 1 1 1 1 1 1 1 1 1 1 1 1 1 1 1 1
 1 1 1 1 1 1 1 1 1 1 1 1 1 1 1 1 2 2 0 2 2 2 2 2 2 2 2 2 2 2 2 2 2 2 2 2
 2 2 2 2 2 2 0 2 2 2 2 2 2 2 2 2 2 2 2 2 2 2 2 2 2 2 2 2 0 2 0 0 0
 0 2 0 0 0 0 0 2 2 0 0 0 2 0 2 0 2 0 0 2 2 0 0 0 0 2 0 0 0 2 0
 0 0 2 0 0 2 0 0 2]
```

> **Note**
>
> This is a simple example. In practice, you would likely spend more time exploring and visualizing the data, tuning the number of clusters, and interpreting the results of the clustering algorithm.

ID3 decision tree

ID3 (Iterative Dichotomiser 3) is a popular algorithm for building decision trees. The ID3 algorithm was developed by Ross Quinlan in 1986 and is based on the concept of information entropy.

The goal of a decision tree is to create a model that can be used to make predictions or classify new instances based on their characteristics. A decision tree consists of a set of nodes and edges, where each node represents a decision or a test on one or more input variables, and each edge represents the possible outcome of that decision.

The ID3 algorithm works by recursively partitioning the data based on the input variables with the highest information gain. Information gain is a measure of the reduction in entropy or impurity that results from splitting the data on a particular input variable. The algorithm selects the input variable that maximizes information gain at each step, until all instances in a given partition belong to the same class or a stopping criterion is met.

The ID3 algorithm has several advantages, including its simplicity and efficiency in handling large datasets with categorical variables. However, it has limitations in handling continuous variables and overfitting, which can be addressed by using modified algorithms such as C4.5 and CART.

In the next example, we can see how ID3 works in practice.

Example

In this example, we are using the following animal-related dataset:

Animal	Has fur?	Has feathers?	Eats meat?	Classification
Dog	Yes	No	Yes	Mammal
Cat	Yes	No	Yes	Mammal
Parrot	No	Yes	No	Bird
Eagle	No	Yes	Yes	Bird
Snake	No	No	Yes	Reptile

Table 2.3: Animal characteristics data

Our goal is to build a decision tree that can classify animals based on their features.

First, let's calculate the entropy of the entire dataset. Entropy measures the impurity of a dataset. A dataset with all the same class labels has an entropy of 0, while a dataset with an equal number of examples from each class has an entropy of 1.

A general equation to calculate entropy can be represented in the the following way:

$$E(S) = -\sum_{i=1}^{n} p_i \log_2 p_i$$

In this equation, $E(S)$ is the entropy of a set S, n is the number of classes in S, and pi is the proportion of the number of elements in S that belong to class i.

In this example, we have $n=3$ classes: Mammal, Bird, and Reptile. The number of animals in each class is as follows:

- Mammal: 2 (Dog, Cat)
- Bird: 2 (Parrot, Eagle)
- Reptile: 1 (Snake)

Therefore, the probabilities are as follows:

- p_{Mammal} = 2/5 = 0.4
- p_{Bird} = 2/5 = 0.4
- $p_{Reptile}$ = 1/5 = 0.2

Substituting these values into the entropy formula, we get the following:

$$E(S) = -\left(0.4\log_2 0.4 + 0.4\log_2 0.4 + 0.2\log_2 0.2\right) \approx 1.52193$$

So the entropy of the "Classification" attribute is approximately 1.52.

Next, let's calculate the information gain of the "Has fur?" attribute. Information gain is a measure of how much a given attribute or feature in a dataset contributes to reducing the uncertainty in the classification of the data. In decision trees, information gain is used to select the best attribute to use for splitting the data at each node of the tree.

The information gain formula is as follows:

$$IG(S, A) = E(S) - \sum_{v \in Values(A)} \frac{|S_v|}{|S|} E(S_v)$$

where A is the attribute (in this case, "Has fur?"), v is a possible value of the attribute, $Values(A)$ is the set of possible values, $|Sv|$ is the number of animals in the dataset that have attribute $A=v$, and $E(Sv)$ is the entropy of the subset of animals that have attribute $A=v$.

We can split the data based on whether the animals have fur or not. The subsets are as follows:

- Has fur: Dog, Cat
- No fur: Parrot, Eagle, Snake

The proportion of animals in each subset is as follows:

- $|S_{Has\ fur}| = 2$
- $|S_{No\ fur}| = 3$

To calculate $E(S_{Has\ fur})$, we need to count the number of animals in each class that have fur:

- Mammal: 2 (Dog, Cat)
- Bird: 0
- Reptile: 0

Therefore, the probabilities are as follows:

- $p_{Mammal} = 1$
- $p_{Bird} = 0$
- $p_{Reptile} = 0$

Substituting these values into the entropy formula, we get the following results:

$$E(S_{Has\ fur}) = -1\log_2 1 = 0$$

Entropy of 0 means that the set is perfectly classified: in this case, all animals with fur are mammals.

To calculate $E(S_{\text{No fur}})$, we need to count the number of animals in each class that don't have fur:

- Mammal: 0
- Bird: 2 (Parrot, Eagle)
- Reptile: 1 (Snake)

Therefore, the probabilities are as follows:

- $p_{\text{Mammal}} = 0$
- $p_{\text{Bird}} = 2/3 \approx 0.67$
- $p_{\text{Reptile}} = 1/3 \approx 0.33$

Substituting these values into the entropy formula, we get the following result:

$$E(S_{\text{No fur}}) = -\left(0 + 0.67\log_2 0.67 + 0.33\log_2 0.33\right) \approx 0.9183$$

Now we can substitute these values into the information gain formula:

$$IG(S, \text{Has fur?}) = E(S) - \sum_{v \in \text{Values(Has fur?)}} \frac{|S_v|}{|S|} E(S_v)$$

$$= 1.52193 - \left(\frac{2}{5} \times 0 + \frac{3}{5} \times 0.9183\right) \approx 0.971$$

Therefore, the information gained for the "Has fur?" attribute is approximately 0.971.

We could also calculate the information gained for the "Has feathers?" and "Eats meat?" attributes by using the same formula and splitting the data based on whether the animals have feathers or not or whether they eat meat or not. The attribute with the highest information gain would be selected to split the data at the root of the decision tree.

Information gain for "Has feathers?" is also 0.971, and for "Eats meat?" it is 0.322. In this case, we will select "Has fur?" for our root node.

Let's take a look at the same example with R and Python. Both code snippets will load the animal dataset, create the decision tree model, visualize it, and test the tree with new data. At the end, we can see that the new animal is classified as Mammal.

The final decision tree looks like the one in the following figure:

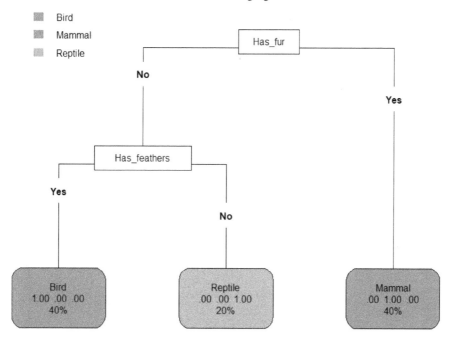

Figure 2.1: Final decision tree (printed using the following R code)

Here is the example with R:

```
data <- data.frame(
  Animal = c("Dog", "Cat", "Parrot", "Eagle", "Snake"),
  Has_fur = c("Yes", "Yes", "No", "No", "No"),
  Has_feathers = c("No", "No", "Yes", "Yes", "No"),
  Eats_meat = c("Yes", "Yes", "No", "Yes", "Yes"),
  Classification = c("Mammal", "Mammal", "Bird", "Bird", "Reptile")
)
library(rpart)
library(rpart.plot)
tree <- rpart(Classification ~ Has_fur + Has_feathers + Eats_meat,
data = data, method = "class", control = rpart.control(minsplit = 1))
rpart.plot(tree, type=5)
new_data <- data.frame(
  Has_fur = "Yes",
  Has_feathers = "No",
  Eats_meat = "Yes"
)
```

```
predicted <- predict(tree, new_data, type = "class")
print(predicted)
```

The Python example is similar to the preceding R example, but in Python, we also need to convert categorical features to numerical using one-hot encoding:

```python
import pandas as pd
import numpy as np
from sklearn.tree import DecisionTreeClassifier, plot_tree
import matplotlib.pyplot as plt
data = pd.DataFrame({
    'Animal': ['Dog', 'Cat', 'Parrot', 'Eagle', 'Snake'],
    'Has_fur': ['Yes', 'Yes', 'No', 'No', 'No'],
    'Has_feathers': ['No', 'No', 'Yes', 'Yes', 'No'],
    'Eats_meat': ['Yes', 'Yes', 'No', 'Yes', 'Yes'],
    'Classification': ['Mammal', 'Mammal', 'Bird', 'Bird', 'Reptile']
})
data_encoded = pd.get_dummies(data[['Has_fur', 'Has_feathers', 'Eats_
meat']])
clf = DecisionTreeClassifier(criterion='entropy', min_samples_split=2)
clf.fit(data_encoded, data['Classification'])
plt.figure(figsize=(8, 6))
plot_tree(clf, feature_names=data_encoded.columns, class_names=np.
unique(data['Classification']), filled=True)
plt.show()
new_data = pd.DataFrame({
    'Has_fur_No': [0],
    'Has_fur_Yes': [1],
    'Has_feathers_No': [1],
    'Has_feathers_Yes': [0],
    'Eats_meat_No': [0],
    'Eats_meat_Yes': [1]
})
predicted = clf.predict(new_data)
print(predicted)
```

> **Note**
> This is a really simple example of a decision tree using the ID3 algorithm. In real-world examples, we would most likely have a lot of data and therefore multiple nodes and branches in our final tree.

We have now learned how clustering algorithms, decision trees, and random forests work. These algorithms are an important part of machine learning and are commonly used for classification. In the next section, we will take a closer look into boosting algorithms and Naive Bayes.

Boosting algorithms and Naive Bayes

Boosting is a machine learning technique that involves creating an ensemble of weak learners to form a strong learner. The idea behind boosting algorithms is to iteratively train models on the data, where each new model attempts to correct the errors of the previous model. Boosting algorithms are widely used in supervised learning tasks, such as classification and regression.

There are several key types of boosting algorithms:

- **AdaBoost (Adaptive Boosting):** AdaBoost is one of the earliest and most popular boosting algorithms. It starts by training a base classifier on the entire dataset and then sequentially trains additional classifiers on the samples that the previous classifiers got wrong. The final prediction is made by taking a weighted sum of the predictions of all the classifiers.

- **Gradient Boosting:** Gradient Boosting is another popular boosting algorithm that works by iteratively adding new models to the ensemble, each trained to minimize the error of the previous models. Gradient Boosting is used in regression and classification problems and has been shown to achieve state-of-the-art results in many applications.

- **XGBoost:** XGBoost (Extreme Gradient Boosting) is a popular and highly optimized implementation of the Gradient Boosting algorithm. XGBoost uses a regularized objective function and a variety of techniques to reduce overfitting and improve accuracy.

Boosting algorithms are known for their ability to improve the accuracy of machine-learning models by reducing bias and variance.

Naive Bayes is a simple but effective algorithm used for classification tasks. It is based on Bayes' theorem, which states that the probability of a hypothesis (in this case, a class label) is updated in the light of new evidence (in this case, the feature values of a new data point). The algorithm assumes that the features are independent of each other, which is why it is called "naïve."

In Naive Bayes, the probability of a data point belonging to a particular class is calculated by multiplying the prior probability of that class by the likelihood of the data point given that class. The algorithm then selects the class with the highest probability as the predicted class for that data point.

There are several variants of the Naive Bayes algorithm:

- **Gaussian Naive Bayes**: Used when the features are continuous and assumed to be normally distributed
- **Multinomial Naive Bayes**: Used when the features are discrete and represent counts or frequencies (such as in text classification)
- **Bernoulli Naive Bayes**: A variant of Multinomial Naive Bayes, used when the features are binary (such as in spam filtering)

Naive Bayes is a simple and efficient algorithm that works well on high-dimensional datasets with sparse features. It is widely used in natural-language processing, spam filtering, sentiment analysis, and other classification tasks. However, the assumption of feature independence may not hold true in all cases, and the algorithm may not perform well if the data violates this assumption.

In the next sections, we will take a closer look into some of the boosting and Naive Bayes algorithms.

XGBoost

XGBoost (eXtreme Gradient Boosting) is an open source machine learning library that is designed to be highly efficient, flexible, and scalable. It is an implementation of gradient-boosting algorithms that can be used for both classification and regression problems.

It is based on the gradient-boosting framework and uses an ensemble of decision trees to make predictions. XGBoost is designed to handle large-scale and high-dimensional data and provides various techniques to prevent overfitting, such as regularization and early stopping.

Let's take a look into simple examples of XGBoost with R and Python. In these examples, we will use the iris dataset that we have already used in earlier chapters of this book. We will split the data into train and test datasets and then train our XGBoost model to predict the species. At the end, we will test the model with our test data and evaluate the model performance.

Here's the example with R:

```
library(xgboost)
library(caret)
data(iris)
set.seed(123)
trainIndex <- createDataPartition(iris$Species, p = 0.8, list = FALSE)
train <- iris[trainIndex, ]
test <- iris[-trainIndex, ]
train$Species <- as.factor(train$Species)
test$Species <- as.factor(test$Species)
train$label <- as.integer(train$Species) - 1
test$label <- as.integer(test$Species) - 1
```

```
xgb_model <- xgboost(data = as.matrix(train[, 1:4]),
                     label = train$label,
                     nrounds = 10,
                     objective = "multi:softmax",
                     num_class = 3,
                     eval_metric = "mlogloss")
predictions <- predict(xgb_model, as.matrix(test[, 1:4]))
predictions <- factor(predictions, levels = 0:2, labels =
levels(iris$Species))
confusionMatrix(predictions, test$Species)
```

Here is the example with Python:

```
import xgboost as xgb
from sklearn.datasets import load_iris
from sklearn.model_selection import train_test_split
from sklearn.metrics import classification_report
iris = load_iris()
X_train, X_test, y_train, y_test = train_test_split(iris.data, iris.
target, test_size=0.2, random_state=123)
xgb_model = xgb.XGBClassifier(objective="multi:softmax",
    n_estimators=10, seed=123)
xgb_model.fit(X_train, y_train)
predictions = xgb_model.predict(X_test)
print(classification_report(y_test, predictions))
```

Gaussian Naive Bayes

Gaussian Naive Bayes (GNB) is a variant of the Naive Bayes algorithm that assumes a Gaussian (normal) distribution for the input variables. In GNB, the probability distribution of each input variable is estimated separately for each class using the training data.

During the testing phase, the model calculates the likelihood of the input features belonging to each class based on the Gaussian distribution parameters estimated during training. Then, the model applies Bayes' theorem to calculate the posterior probability of each class, given the input features. The class with the highest posterior probability is then assigned to the input.

GNB is called "naïve" because it makes a strong assumption that the input features are conditionally independent, given the class label. This assumption simplifies the model and makes the computation of the posterior probabilities tractable. However, this assumption may not hold in practice for some datasets, and thus, the model may not perform well. Nonetheless, GNB can be a fast and accurate classifier for datasets where the independence assumption holds.

Let's take a look into a similar classification problem, as we did with XGBoost, using Gaussian Naive Bayes. Here is the example code with both R and Python. Once again, we are using the iris dataset to classify the different species.

Here is the example with R:

```
library(e1071)
data(iris)
set.seed(123)
trainIndex <- sample(nrow(iris), 0.7 * nrow(iris))
train <- iris[trainIndex, ]
test <- iris[-trainIndex, ]
model <- naiveBayes(Species ~ ., data = train)
predictions <- predict(model, test)
cfm <- table(predictions, test$Species)
print(cfm)
```

Here is the example with Python:

```
from sklearn.datasets import load_iris
from sklearn.model_selection import train_test_split
from sklearn.naive_bayes import GaussianNB
from sklearn.metrics import classification_report
iris = load_iris()
X_train, X_test, y_train, y_test = train_test_split(iris.data,
        iris.target, test_size=0.3, random_state=123)
model = GaussianNB()
model.fit(X_train, y_train)
predictions = model.predict(X_test)
print(classification_report(y_test, predictions))
```

Now we have familiarized ourselves with the concepts of boosting algorithms and Naive Bayes. These methods are used widely in Qlik AutoML, and understanding the concepts of these algorithms is an essential skill to work with machine-learning problems. In our next section, we will take a closer look at some of the advanced machine-learning algorithms, including neural networks, deep learning, and natural-language models.

Neural networks, deep learning, and natural-language models

Neural networks are a type of machine-learning algorithm that is inspired by the structure and function of the human brain. They are composed of layers of interconnected nodes or artificial neurons that process and transmit information.

In a neural network, the input data is fed into the first layer of nodes, which applies a set of mathematical transformations to the data and produces an output. The output of the first layer is then fed into the second layer, which applies another set of transformations to produce another output, and so on until the final output is produced.

The connections between the nodes in the neural network have weights that are adjusted during the learning process to optimize the network's ability to make accurate predictions or classifications. This is typically achieved using an optimization algorithm such as stochastic gradient descent. An example of the structure of a neural network is visualized in the following figure:

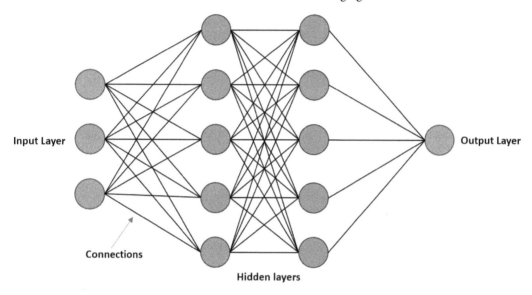

Figure 2.2: High-level architecture of a neural network

Neural networks have been used to solve a wide range of machine-learning problems, including image and speech recognition, natural language processing, and predictive modeling. They have been shown to be effective in many applications due to their ability to learn complex, non-linear relationships between input and output data.

Deep learning involves the use of neural networks with multiple layers. It has achieved significant success in a wide range of applications, including computer vision, speech recognition, natural-language processing, and game playing. Some notable examples include the use of deep learning in image recognition tasks, such as identifying objects in photos, and in natural language processing tasks, such as language translation and sentiment analysis.

One of the key advantages of deep learning is its ability to automatically learn features from data without the need for manual feature engineering. This makes it possible to train models on large datasets with many features, which can be computationally challenging or even impossible with traditional machine learning methods.

However, training deep neural networks can also be challenging due to the large number of parameters and the risk of overfitting. To address these challenges, researchers have developed a variety of techniques, including regularization methods, dropout, and batch normalization, that can improve the performance and stability of deep neural networks.

Natural-language models are a type of machine-learning model that can process and understand human language. These models are trained on large amounts of text data, such as books, articles, and social media posts, and learn to generate coherent and semantically meaningful responses to natural language input.

One common type of natural-language model is the language model, which is trained to predict the probability of a sequence of words given a context. For example, a language model might be trained to predict the probability of the word "pizza," given the context "I am in the mood for something to eat that is typically round and covered in toppings."

Another type of natural-language model is the text-generation model, which can be used to generate natural-language text, such as news articles, stories, and chatbot responses. These models can be trained to generate text that is similar to a particular style or genre, or even to imitate the writing style of a particular author.

Natural-language models have a wide range of applications, including language translation, sentiment analysis, chatbots and virtual assistants, and text summarization. Recent advances in deep learning and natural language processing have led to the development of powerful language models such as GPT-3, which can generate coherent and human-like text on a wide range of topics. Qlik Insight Advisor is one example of a product that has integrated the natural-language model.

Summary

In this chapter, we have gained an overview of different machine-learning algorithms. We have discovered how different algorithms can be used to solve problems and how they function. We started this chapter by getting familiar with some of the most common regression algorithms and gained knowledge on how to use these in R and Python. We discovered how to utilize clustering, decision trees, and random forests with practical examples.

In the later part of this chapter, we moved on to more complex algorithms and learned how different boosting algorithms, neural networks, and other advanced models function. These models are utilized in Qlik AutoML, and it's important to know how each model is structured. After reading this chapter, you now have a basic understanding of the models and are prepared to utilize these with Qlik tools. We will use most of these algorithms in the later parts of this book.

In the next chapter, we will focus on data literacy in a machine-learning context. Data literacy is a hot topic, and it is also an important concept in the world of machine learning. To be able to create a well-functioning model and interpret the results from it, we must be able to understand the data. This is where data literacy comes into play.

3
Data Literacy in a Machine Learning Context

As we enter the age of artificial intelligence and machine learning, it's becoming increasingly important to develop a foundational understanding of data literacy. In this chapter, we will explore the concept of data literacy and its critical role in the world of machine learning.

Data literacy refers to the ability to read, analyze, and understand data. With the rapid growth of data in our daily lives, data literacy has become a crucial skill for individuals, businesses, and organizations alike. In the context of machine learning, data literacy is especially important, as it forms the backbone of the entire process.

Machine learning models are only as good as the data they're trained on, and data literacy plays a vital role in ensuring that the data used for training is of high quality, relevant, and free of bias.

In this chapter, we're going to cover the following main topics:

- Data literacy and the skills required to be data literate
- Informed decision-making and methods to make informed decisions
- Data strategy and how to utilize data efficiently in organizations

What is data literacy?

As stated previously, data literacy refers to the ability to read, analyze, and understand data. It encompasses a range of skills, including the ability to read and interpret data visualizations, understand statistical concepts, and apply critical thinking to data analysis. Data literacy is becoming increasingly important in today's data-driven world, as individuals and organizations are faced with ever-growing amounts of data that need to be analyzed and interpreted in order to make informed decisions.

In many fields, such as business, healthcare, and government, data literacy has become a crucial skill, and it's also vital in the field of machine learning, where models are only as good as the data they are trained on.

Data literacy is not just about technical skills, but also includes the ability to critically evaluate data and identify potential biases or limitations. It involves a mindset of curiosity, skepticism, and a willingness to ask questions and seek answers. Ultimately, data literacy enables individuals and organizations to make more informed decisions and drive meaningful change.

Some of the key skills included in data literacy are as follows:

- **Data collection:** The ability to identify and gather data from various sources, including databases, APIs, surveys, and other sources

- **Data cleaning:** The ability to clean and preprocess data to ensure it is accurate, consistent, and in a usable format for analysis

- **Data analysis:** The ability to analyze and interpret data using statistical methods, data visualization techniques, machine learning, and other tools

- **Data visualization:** The ability to create visual representations of data to facilitate understanding and communication

- **Effective communication:** The ability to communicate insights and findings from data analysis to others in a clear and concise manner

- **Ethics:** An understanding of the ethical implications of working with data, including issues such as privacy, security, and bias

- **Technical skills:** Proficiency with tools and technologies used for data analysis, such as programming languages (e.g., Python, R), statistical software (e.g., SAS, SPSS), and data visualization tools (e.g., Qlik)

- **Critical thinking:** The ability to evaluate data critically and identify potential biases, limitations, and errors

- **Domain knowledge:** Knowledge of the field or industry in which the data is being used, to understand the context of the data and its potential uses

So basically, data literacy skills can be divided into technical and non-technical skills. Let's take a closer look at some of the most essential skills next. We will start with non-technical skills first.

Critical thinking

Critical thinking is one of the most important skills when working with data. In data literacy, critical thinking refers to the ability to evaluate data in a systematic and objective manner, considering potential biases, limitations, and errors. It involves questioning assumptions, analyzing evidence, and making informed judgments about the quality and reliability of the data. It also involves assessing the limitations of the analysis and recognizing the potential for false conclusions or overgeneralizations based on incomplete or insufficient data.

One aspect of critical thinking is considering the broader context in which the data is being used. This includes understanding the goals of the analysis, the intended audience, and the potential implications of the findings. Skills developed in this area will help you to think analytically and draw conclusions that can lead to insights and actions. In a machine-learning context, this skill will help you to understand how to ask proper questions and how to create a suitable model for your analysis.

In general, there are some habits that can be used to develop critical-thinking skills. First, you should question all assumptions and not take anything for granted. This way, you can start to develop a habit that can give you new ideas and perspective. You should also seek out diversity. This means simply ensuring that you discuss with other people and hear their views. This habit will make you better at recognizing biases that might represent your own point of view.

Lastly, you should use pure logic when making decisions. It is a good idea to reason through each step to make sure that you understand the logic behind everything you do. For example, when planning a machine-learning deployment, it is always a good idea to go through each step of your plan and share the process and results with other people.

Research and domain knowledge

Most of the time, you might have a comprehensive domain knowledge from the field you are working in, but sometimes being data literate in a certain topic will require research and studying. This could be, for example, cross-checking the results you get from your machine-learning model or simply finding good source data.

Another aspect of research is that it helps you to stay up to date with the latest developments and best practices in the field. With the rapid growth of data and the increasing importance of data-driven decision-making, there is always something to learn, and it is important to keep pace with new technologies, tools, and methods.

There is also an ethical aspect involved. Research skills are essential for addressing ethical considerations related to working with data, such as privacy concerns, biases, and the responsible use of data. By conducting research on these topics, you can ensure that you are using data in an ethical and responsible manner and contribute to the development of ethical guidelines and best practices.

Research means a lot more than using a search engine. It involves finding good sources and cross-referencing them. It also involves drawing conclusions and evaluating those carefully after the project is done. One method for efficient research is narrowing down. You can start with a broad approach and dig deeper into some of the topics. Never start researching with an outcome already in your mind and keep your mind open. Make sure to verify your sources.

Combining research with domain knowledge that you have already acquired from previous experiences is an important skill. This approach will allow you to ask relevant questions, identify key variables, and interpret the data in a meaningful way. Combining research, domain knowledge, effective communication, and technical skills can help you to develop a strong foundation for working with data and machine learning effectively in your field or industry.

Communication

Individual skills in data literacy are important but it's equally important to be able to communicate the data and findings to other people. Effective communication allows you to communicate insights and findings from data analysis in a clear, concise, and meaningful way. It involves not only presenting the data in a clear and understandable manner but also providing context and interpretation that can help the audience to understand the implications and potential uses of the data.

Communication is also important for building trust and credibility with the audience. By presenting data in a clear and transparent manner, you can build trust and increase the likelihood that the audience will use the data to inform their decisions. Different audiences may have different levels of technical knowledge and they may be interested in different aspects of the data. By understanding the audience and tailoring the message to their needs, you can increase the effectiveness of your communication and ensure that the audience is able to understand and make use of the data and findings. In a machine learning context, it is crucial to create trust and provide clear communication about the possibilities and limitations of each solution.

It is important to make sure that your audience and colleagues are on the same page as you, especially if they are involved in creating the machine-learning models or analyzing the results. Misunderstandings may lead to critical problems and business implications.

To improve communication skills, there are several strategies that can be applied specifically to communicating about data. First and foremost, practice is key. The more you practice communicating about data, the more comfortable and confident you will become. It's also important to know the audience and understand their level of knowledge, goals, and interests. Using plain language, providing context, and using visuals such as graphs and charts can make complex data easier to understand and more engaging.

Telling a story can help make the data more compelling and memorable. It's also important to practice active listening and respond to feedback from the audience in a thoughtful and respectful manner. Seeking feedback from trusted colleagues, mentors, or advisors can help you identify areas for improvement and refine your communication skills over time.

Technical skills

Technical skills are a fundamental aspect of data literacy, as they enable individuals to effectively work with data using various technical tools and platforms. Technical skills encompass a broad range of competencies, including data collection, cleaning, analysis, visualization, programming, database management, data modeling, machine learning, and data security and privacy.

Data collection involves the ability to gather data from various sources, including databases, websites, APIs, and other data repositories. Data cleaning and preparation are crucial for eliminating errors, inconsistencies, and missing values in raw data and making it ready for analysis. Data analysis includes utilizing statistical methods, machine-learning algorithms, and other analytical techniques to recognize patterns, trends, and insights within data. Data visualization is the process of creating visual representations of data using graphs, charts, and other visualizations to make data more understandable and actionable.

Other technical skills can include, for example, programming, database management and data modeling. Technical skills enable individuals to work with data more effectively, develop accurate predictions and insights, and communicate their findings in a way that is easily understood by their audience. Since most of the content of this book is related to technical skills, we are not going deeper into individual skills in this chapter.

The following figure summarizes the key skills of being data literate:

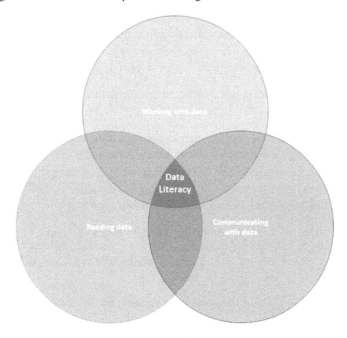

Figure 3.1: Three areas of being data literate

In this section, we familiarized ourselves with the concept of data literacy. Next, we will take a closer look at informed decision-making and how to use data literacy skills to support decision-making.

Informed decision-making

Informed decision-making refers to the process of using data to make decisions that are supported by evidence and grounded in a thorough understanding of the data. It involves the ability to identify relevant data, analyze it using appropriate tools and techniques, and draw conclusions that are based on evidence rather than assumptions or intuition. Informed decision-making is a critical skill for individuals who work with data, as it allows them to leverage data to drive better outcomes and make decisions that are backed by evidence.

To make informed decisions, you must have a clear understanding of the problem or question at hand, as well as the data that is relevant to it. You must be able to identify appropriate data sources, assess the quality of the data, and choose appropriate analytical techniques to analyze it. Informed decision-making also requires you to be able to interpret the results of your analysis and communicate findings effectively to others.

Informed decision-making is particularly important in industries where decisions can have significant consequences, such as healthcare, finance, and government. For example, healthcare professionals may use data to make informed decisions about patient care and treatment, while financial analysts may use data to make investment decisions.

Informed decision-making is not just about using data to make decisions, but also about using data to evaluate the effectiveness of those decisions. This requires organizations to be able to monitor and measure the outcomes of decisions and use this feedback to refine the decision-making process over time.

Ultimately, informed decision-making is the ability to transform information into actions and base all decisions on knowledge.

There are many models for informed decision-making in organizations. The one we are going to see here combines the need to ask the right questions, source the correct data in the right format, critically analyze and evaluate the data, apply the domain knowledge of yourself and others (being conscious about potential biases), and communicate the decision to all relevant stakeholders. There is also a mechanism to monitor and iterate the process to make it better over time.

Let's take a closer look at the process. We can divide it into 12 different steps:

1. **Ask:** Turn your business questions into analytical questions. Draft your questions for machine learning. What is the target outcome you are aiming for?

2. **Acquire:** Find all relevant data. Remember to utilize both the internal and public data available and relevant to your problem.

3. Ensure that you have all the needed data available and cross check that it can be trusted. Make sure that it's in right format. Utilize profiling, scaling, tagging, standardization, and catalog features. Make sure you have handled sensitive data correctly.

4. **Analyze:** Create a proper analysis and visualizations to describe your data, with KPIs.

5. **Find patterns and trends:** Try to plot relationships and drill deeper into data. Start thinking about your original question. Can it be solved and is it still relevant?

6. **Apply:** Review what you have achieved so far and start applying your domain knowledge to the results.

7. **Challenge your findings and data:** Look for any evidence that gives you a reason to disprove your earlier findings.

8. **Review the results with your team and colleagues:** If you are working alone, try to take another look and find possible bias.

9. **Start leveraging machine learning:** Run multiple simulations and build multiple models. Test all solutions carefully and review the results. Augment your earlier analysis with the results.

10. **Announce:** Communicate your findings and results to your organization. Make sure to present them to the right audience. Use different levels of detail for different stakeholders.

11. **Access:** Set up a mechanism to review your work. Monitor the effects of the decisions made.

12. Leverage all feedback collected and iterate your process. Try to fail fast and fix the issues instantly. Document your findings and how these have altered the original process.

Developing a good process for you and your organization can take time and multiple iterations but it will greatly benefit both individuals and the organization over time. When decisions are based on facts and data, they are easier to justify and will guide you to the correct path more often than decisions based on only partial information or a feeling.

Over a longer period, having a refined decision-making process will lead to reduced risk, increased efficiency, better resource allocation, improved communication, and competitive advantage.

In this section, we investigated the methods of informed decision-making and how to make informed decisions at an organizational level. In the next section, we will move towards the larger picture and focus on data strategy.

Data strategy

Data strategy is a crucial element of any organization's overall strategy, as it enables organizations to leverage data to achieve their objectives. A well-designed data strategy considers the organization's goals, challenges, and available resources and outlines the steps needed to collect, manage, analyze, and use data effectively.

One of the key components of a data strategy is data governance, which establishes policies and procedures for data management and usage across the organization. Data governance includes defining data ownership, establishing data standards, and ensuring compliance with data regulations. By having a clear understanding of data governance, organizations can ensure that data is being used ethically and securely, which builds trust with stakeholders.

Well-defined data architecture is another cornerstone of a working data strategy. Data architecture involves designing the structure and systems for managing and storing data. This includes defining data models, selecting appropriate database technologies, and ensuring data integration across systems. By having a robust data architecture in place, organizations can ensure that data is accessible, accurate, and consistent, which improves decision-making and operational efficiency.

Data analytics and machine learning can be seen as core technologies to leverage data strategy. This involves using various techniques to extract insights from data using predictive modeling, machine learning, and data visualization platforms. By using data analytics to gain insights, organizations can make more informed decisions, identify new opportunities, and improve business processes.

Data quality is essential in a data strategy, as it ensures that data is accurate, complete, and consistent. This includes establishing data quality standards, performing data validation, and cleansing data as needed. By ensuring data quality, organizations can trust the data they are using for decision-making, which reduces the risk of making errors and improves operational efficiency.

Security and data ownership are key components of every working data strategy. Data security ensures that data is protected from unauthorized access and cyber threats. This includes implementing data security policies, using encryption technologies, and establishing access controls. By securing data, organizations can prevent data breaches, which protects their reputation and reduces the risk of financial and legal penalties.

Having clear ownership for all the data assets will make it transparent who has the right to approve the usage of data and make updates or modifications to datasets. The data steward or owner also works as a domain expert of the data assets and can be a point of contact for data-related questions inside the organization.

When creating a data strategy for an organization, there are some key principles to follow. The basics of a working data strategy involve understanding the key components and designing a plan that aligns with the organization's goals, challenges, and available resources.

Some of the basics of a working data strategy include the following:

- Understanding the organization's goals: A data strategy should align with the organization's overall goals and objectives. This involves understanding what the organization wants to achieve and how data can support those goals.

- Defining data governance: Data governance is critical to ensuring that data is managed and used ethically and securely. This involves defining data ownership, establishing data standards, and ensuring compliance with data regulations.

- Establishing data architecture: A well-designed data architecture is essential to managing and storing data effectively. This involves defining data models, selecting appropriate database technologies, and ensuring data integration across systems.

- Using data analytics: Data analytics is critical to extracting insights from data and making informed decisions. This involves using various techniques such as predictive modeling, machine learning, and data visualization.

- Ensuring data quality: Data quality is critical to ensuring that data is accurate, complete, and consistent. This involves establishing data quality standards, performing data validation, and cleansing data as needed.

- Securing data: Data security is critical to protecting data from unauthorized access and cyber threats. This involves implementing data security policies, using encryption technologies, and establishing access controls.

- Monitoring and adapting: A data strategy should be monitored regularly to ensure that it remains aligned with the organization's goals and is delivering the expected benefits. It may need to be adapted as the organization's goals, challenges, or available resources change.

The following figure summarizes the key pillars of a data strategy:

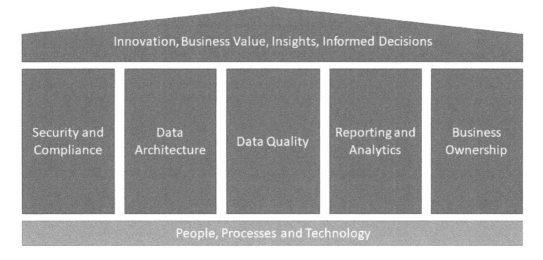

Figure 3.2: Pillars of a data strategy

Evaluating the maturity of the current data strategy is a good starting point for improvements. The existing data strategy should be constantly evaluated. To evaluate the maturity of an organization's data strategy, it is necessary to assess the extent to which it aligns with its goals and objectives, and its ability to execute the strategy effectively. This involves defining the key criteria that are relevant to evaluating the maturity, such as data governance policies, data architecture, data analytics capabilities, data quality metrics, and data security guidance.

The next step is to assess the organization's current data strategy against the identified criteria. This may involve reviewing existing documentation, interviewing stakeholders, and performing data analysis. Based on this assessment, any gaps or areas of improvement that need to be addressed to improve the maturity of the data strategy should be identified.

A roadmap for improving the maturity of the data strategy can then be developed based on the assessment and gap analysis. This roadmap should include specific action items, timelines, and resources required to implement the roadmap. Regular monitoring of the progress of the data strategy implementation is necessary, and adjustments to the roadmap may be needed as the organization's goals or data-related challenges change.

By regularly evaluating the maturity of a data strategy, it is possible to identify areas of improvement and develop a roadmap for improving the organization's capabilities.

There are many maturity models for organizations. Next, we are going to take a brief look at one model that combines multiple common approaches into one.

This model describes the organization's maturity using four steps:

1. The organization is just getting started with a data strategy. They use mainly internal data and ad hoc analysis. There are no analytics in place or only simple descriptive analytics are used. Static reports and spreadsheets are common tools.

2. The organization recognizes the importance of a data strategy. They are making insightful business decisions and care about the quality of data. Analysis can include diagnostic use cases and there is typically a BI platform.

3. The organization uses data as described in the previous step, but they are augmenting the use cases and using external data to complement the internal data. Use cases can include predictive analysis and machine learning. There is a data strategy in action and decisions are mainly based on an informed decision-making model.

4. At the highest level of the organization are the leaders and innovators when it comes to using data. They are staying on top of the latest trends and use data in innovative ways. They are developing machine-learning models and utilizing prescriptive analytics to automatically prescribe the best course of action. They are constantly iterating the current data strategy and adapting new ways of working. Roles and the organizational structure support the comprehensive usage of data.

Creating a data strategy and transforming the organization from the first level of maturity to a data innovator is a long-term project and is not further discussed in this book. There is a lot of material written about data strategy and it is highly recommended to also consider the bigger picture when working with data and utilizing machine learning in your organization.

Summary

In this chapter, we first learned what data literacy means as a concept. We investigated the methods of being data literate and discussed how to apply these methods to our work. Being able to read and utilize data is an important skill in the modern world, since there is an increasing amount of data around us all the time.

We discovered what informed decision-making is and went through the process of making informed decisions with data, analytics, and machine learning. This process will be our guiding light in the next chapter when we are starting to lean towards the practice. It will give us guidelines that we will use to form our machine-learning question and when we are defining the solution.

At the end of this chapter, we briefly discussed data strategy and maturity. Data strategy is an important aspect of every modern organization but is also a wide topic. We scratched the surface of how to define the maturity of an organization from a data point of view and what are the most important aspects of a data strategy.

In the next chapter, we will start to focus on a practical approach to solving problems with machine learning. We will go through the steps required to create a good machine learning solution with the Qlik platform. We will cover how to define a problem and select a model, how to prepare the data, and what to consider when visualizing the end results.

4

Creating a Good Machine Learning Solution with the Qlik Platform

This chapter provides an overview of the key steps involved in creating effective machine learning solutions with Qlik. The same principles apply to all machine learning tools and solutions.

The process starts with defining the problem to be solved and aligning it with the organization's goals. Data preparation is critical and Qlik provides robust data preparation capabilities for collecting, cleaning, and transforming data to ensure its quality and relevance.

Data exploration and visualization using Qlik's features are essential for understanding data patterns and informing the machine learning model. Model selection is crucial and Qlik offers a wide range of algorithms for different use cases.

Once the model is selected, it needs to be trained using the corresponding tools. Model evaluation using appropriate metrics helps assess its performance and make necessary refinements.

Deployment of the model within the Qlik environment involves integration into apps or dashboards, creating APIs, or embedding it into web applications. Monitoring and maintenance of the deployed model ensures its accuracy and relevance over time. Interpretation and communication of results are key for driving decision-making. Qlik's visualization and reporting capabilities enable effective communication of insights to stakeholders.

Here is what you will learn as a part of this chapter:

- How to define a machine learning problem and select the correct model to solve it
- Steps needed to clean and prepare data
- How to prepare and validate the machine learning model
- How to effectively visualize and communicate the end results

Defining a machine learning problem

Defining a machine learning problem involves identifying a specific business challenge or analytical objective that can be addressed using machine learning techniques. The process of defining a problem can be divided into a few key steps:

1. **Understand the business objective**: Start by gaining a clear understanding of the overall business objective or problem that needs to be solved. This could be improving customer retention, optimizing pricing strategies, predicting equipment failures, or identifying potential fraud cases, among others.

2. **Identify the key problem or challenge**: Once the business objective is defined, identify the specific problem or challenge that needs to be addressed using machine learning. This involves understanding the key pain points, limitations, or gaps in the current process or system that can be improved through machine learning.

3. **Define the scope and boundaries**: Clearly define the scope and boundaries of the machine learning problem. This includes determining the specific data inputs and outputs, the timeframe of the problem, and any constraints or limitations in terms of data availability, resources, or feasibility.

4. **Formulate the problem statement**: Craft a clear and concise problem statement that describes the business challenge or objective in a specific and measurable way. The problem statement should be well defined and measurable, allowing for objective evaluation of the machine learning solution's success.

5. **Consider the data requirements**: Analyze the data requirements for the machine learning problem. Identify the relevant data sources, data types, and data quality requirements. Consider the availability, completeness, and accuracy of data, as well as any data privacy or security considerations.

6. **Define the evaluation metrics**: Define the evaluation metrics that will be used to assess the performance of the machine learning solution. These metrics should align with the problem statement and business objective and provide a quantitative measure of the solution's success.

7. **Consider the feasibility and impact**: Evaluate the feasibility and potential impact of the machine learning solution. Consider the technical feasibility of implementing the solution, the availability of necessary resources, and the expected impact on the business objective or problem being addressed.

By following these steps, you can effectively define a machine learning problem and lay the foundation for building a successful machine learning solution. Clear problem definition is crucial for guiding the entire machine learning process, from data preparation to model training, evaluation, and deployment.

Note

Qlik uses a four-step framework to help define machine learning problems. The framework consists of the following steps:

1. Event trigger

    Example: Customer places an order

2. Target

    Example: Another order is placed within one year (Yes | No)

3. Features

    Examples: Age, State, Number of previous orders, Shipping type

4. Prediction point

    Example: One month after order

The framework described here is an extended and more comprehensive version of this framework. This framework can be seen in use in *Chapter 10*.

If we are going to use Qlik AutoML for our model creation, it is important to remember that the following scenarios are supported:

*   **Binary classification**: This applies to any question that can be answered with *Yes* or *No*. Examples: *Will my customer churn? Will my inventory stock run out? Will my patient cancel their appointment?*

Note

Optimally, we want to turn every machine learning question into a binary classification problem if possible since it will deliver the best accuracy in most cases. However, in some cases, we will get better results using other types of algorithms. It is important to choose the correct algorithm based on the problem we are solving.

The binary classification problem can be described with the following diagram:

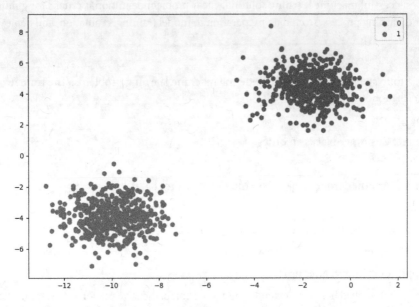

Figure 4.1: Binary classification

- **Multi-class classification**: Questions where there are multiple possible outcomes. Examples: *What product will the customer purchase? What facility will a patient be discharged to?*

The multi-class classification problem can be illustrated as in the following figure:

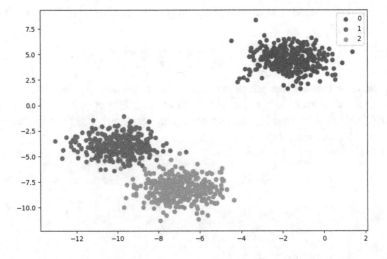

Figure 4.2: Multi-class classification

- **Regression**: This involves the prediction of a value at a future point. Examples: *What will our sales be at the end of the year? What is the expected waiting time for a patient?*

  Regression can be visualized as in the following figure:

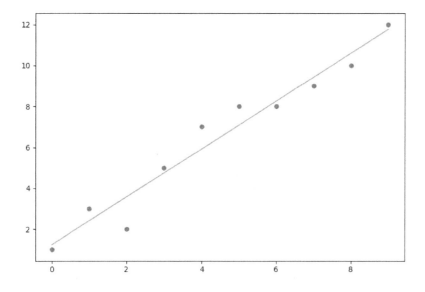

Figure 4.3: Regression

> **Note**
>
> Other use cases can be solved with the Advanced Analytics integration and tools including R, Python, AWS SageMaker, or Azure ML Studio. We will cover setting up these environments in the next chapter.

We have now investigated the basics of forming a machine learning problem and what kind of problems Qlik AutoML can be used to help us solve. In the next section, we will look at the common data preparation steps required for most tasks in machine learning.

Cleaning and preparing data

Data preparation is a crucial step in machine learning because the quality, relevance, and suitability of the data used for model training directly impact the accuracy, reliability, and effectiveness of the resulting machine learning models.

General data preparation steps include the following:

- **Removing null values**
- **Removing columns that are not needed**
- **Encoding (for example, the one-hot encoding that we used in some of the examples in Chapter 2)**
- **Feature scaling**
- **Splitting into test and training datasets**
- Setting correct data types
- Removing duplicates
- Correcting data errors
- Removing outliers

Those steps that are automatically taken care of by Qlik AutoML are shown in **bold** in the preceding list. The rest of the steps can be done in Qlik Sense.

Let's take a closer look at some of these steps using examples.

Example 1 – one-hot encoding

Let's assume that we have the following dataset:

ID	Category	Carnivore
1	Mammal	No
2	Bird	No
3	Mammal	Yes
4	Reptile	No
5	Reptile	Yes

Table 4.1: Example dataset

If we one-hot encode the preceding table, it will look like this:

ID	Mammal	Reptile	Bird	Carnivore
1	1	0	0	No
2	0	0	1	No
3	1	0	0	Yes
4	0	1	0	No
5	0	1	0	Yes

Table 4.2: One-hot encoded example

Here is some example code that achieves the preceding result using Python:

```
import pandas as pd
from sklearn.preprocessing import OneHotEncoder
data = {
    'ID': [1, 2, 3, 4, 5],
    'Category': ['Mammal', 'Bird', 'Mammal', 'Reptile', 'Reptile'],
    'Carnivore': ['No', 'No', 'Yes', 'No', 'Yes']
}
df = pd.DataFrame(data)
encoder = OneHotEncoder(sparse=False)
category_encoded = encoder.fit_transform(df[['Category']])
category_names = encoder.get_feature_names_out(['Category'])
df[category_names] = category_encoded
df.drop('Category', axis=1, inplace=True)
print(df)
```

In the preceding example, the OneHotEncoder from scikit-learn is used to perform one-hot encoding on the Category column. The resulting one-hot encoded values are then added as new columns to the DataFrame, with each category represented as a binary value (1 or 0) in its respective column.

Example 2 – feature scaling

Feature scaling is important in machine learning to ensure that all features or variables have similar scales, as it can affect the performance and convergence of many machine learning algorithms. Min-max scaling is one of the methods commonly used for feature scaling, where the values are scaled to a specific range, usually between 0 and 1.

Let's assume that we have the following dataset:

ID	Age	Income
1	25	50000
2	30	60000
3	35	70000
4	40	80000
5	45	90000

Table 4.3: Example dataset

After feature scaling, we will get the following output:

ID	Age	Income
1	0.00	0.00
2	0.25	0.20
3	0.50	0.40
4	0.75	0.60
5	1.00	0.80

Table 4.4: Example dataset after feature scaling

Here is some Python code to achieve the preceding scaling:

```
import pandas as pd
from sklearn.preprocessing import MinMaxScaler
data = {
    'ID': [1, 2, 3, 4, 5],
    'Age': [25, 30, 35, 40, 45],
    'Income': [50000, 60000, 70000, 80000, 90000]
}
df = pd.DataFrame(data)
scaler = MinMaxScaler()
df[['Age', 'Income']] = scaler.fit_transform(df[['Age', 'Income']])
print(df)
```

In the preceding example, MinMaxScaler from scikit-learn is used to perform feature scaling on the Age and Income columns of the DataFrame. The fit_transform method is called on the selected columns to scale the values between 0 and 1, based on the minimum and maximum values in each column. The resulting scaled values are then updated in the original DataFrame.

The functionality of the preceding example is automatically taken care of by Qlik AutoML but when you are using the Advanced Analytics integration these steps should be considered. The examples reviewed so far in this chapter were written with Python but the same functionality can be also achieved using Qlik scripting or other data manipulation methods. Additionally, null encoding, data type handling, and many other data preparation tasks can be done in Qlik. We will take a closer look at these in *Chapter 6*.

Now that we have familiarized ourselves with the common data cleaning and preprocessing steps, let's examine model preparation and validation. These aspects are important to gain trust in our model and evaluate the results.

Preparing and validating a model

In *Chapter 1*, we discovered some of the concepts for model validation and preparation. Qlik AutoML handles model selection automatically and provides us with comprehensive information to support the validation. We will consider model selection and validation in more detail in *Chapter 7* and Qlik AutoML in *Chapter 8*. In this section, we will prepare for these chapters by summarizing the most important steps of model preparation and validation in Qlik. The following steps are written on Qlik AutoML point of view. When using the Advanced Analytics integration there might be small differences based on the selected technology (ie. R, Python, Azure ML Studio, AWS SageMaker, etc.).

General validation and preparation steps include the following:

- **Data preparation**: Start by preparing your data for machine learning. Load your data into Qlik Sense, clean and preprocess it, handle missing values, and perform feature engineering if necessary. Qlik AutoML supports various data types, including numeric, categorical, and textual data.

- **Model selection**: Choose the appropriate machine learning algorithm for your problem. Qlik AutoML offers a wide range of algorithms, including decision trees, random forests, gradient boosting, support vector machines, and more. You can select multiple algorithms to be evaluated simultaneously for model comparison.

- **Model training**: Once you have selected the algorithms, Qlik AutoML automatically trains multiple models with different hyperparameter configurations. The models are trained on a portion of your data using cross-validation, which helps to evaluate their performance and select the best-performing model.

- **Model evaluation**: After the models are trained, Qlik AutoML provides comprehensive model evaluation metrics such as accuracy, AUC, and F1 score to assess the performance of each model. You can compare the performance of different models and select the one that performs best on your data.

- **Model deployment**: Once you have chosen the best model, you can deploy it in your Qlik Sense app. Qlik AutoML generates the necessary code to implement the model in your app, making it easy to integrate the model into your analytics workflow.

- **Model monitoring**: Qlik AutoML allows you to monitor the performance of your deployed model in real time. You can track key performance metrics and take necessary actions if the model's performance deteriorates over time.

- **Model validation**: Finally, it's important to validate the performance of your deployed model using real-world data. Monitor the model's predictions and compare them with actual outcomes to ensure that the model is making accurate and reliable predictions in a real-world setting.

In this section, we have covered the methods of model preparation and validation in general. The final piece of the machine learning project is typically visualization of the end results. Let's cover the general principles of that in the next section.

Visualizing the end results

When visualizing the end results, we have several options to consider in separate parts of the machine learning solution creation. We will take a deeper look into visualization techniques and different chart types in *Chapter 9*. However, here are some general steps to consider:

- **Load data**: Load your machine learning results data into Qlik Sense either using data sources or direct connection to Qlik AutoML or third-party machine learning platforms. This data can include predicted values, actual values, model evaluation metrics, and other relevant information.

- **Create visualizations**: Use Qlik Sense's built-in visualization tools to create visual representations of your machine learning results. You can choose from various chart types depending on the type of data and the insights you want to convey. Planning a clean and visually appealing user interface is an important step.

- **Customize visualizations**: Customize the appearance and properties of your visualizations to make them visually appealing and informative. Try to select the best possible components to enhance the readability and ease of understanding of your machine learning results. Augment graphical information with written explanations if needed.

- **Share and collaborate**: Share your machine learning results visualizations with relevant stakeholders, such as team members, managers, or clients, using Qlik Sense's sharing and collaboration features. You can publish visualizations to a Qlik Sense app, embed them in other applications, or export them in various formats such as PDF, image, or HTML for easy sharing and dissemination. Utilizing Qlik Alerting, Notes, Storytelling, and other advanced features is encouraged.

Planning the visualizations and communicating results effectively is an important part of driving user adoption of your machine learning solution. By leveraging the visualization capabilities of Qlik Sense, you can effectively communicate and showcase your machine learning results in a visually compelling and interactive manner, enabling users to gain insights and make informed decisions based on the outcomes of your machine learning models.

In the following screenshot, we can see one example of a Qlik Sense dashboard used to visualize results from a Qlik AutoML model:

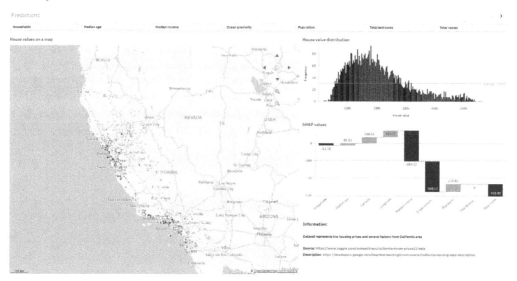

Figure 4.4: Example dashboard visualizing results from Qlik AutoML

Summary

In this chapter, we started to move a bit closer to implementing a machine learning solution with Qlik tools. We discovered the importance of forming a correct business question to be solved and what aspects should be considered when forming a problem.

We discovered some general steps of data preparation and how these should be handled. More detailed techniques for data modeling and transformations are introduced in *Chapter 6*. We also investigated the concept of model preparation and validation briefly.

At the end of this chapter, we discussed the importance of presentation and what to consider when visualizing results with Qlik. This topic is considered in more detail in *Chapter 9*.

In the next chapter, we are going to find out how to prepare environments for our machine learning solutions. We will install on-premises integration for R and Python, discover how to utilize APIs and Advanced Analytics integration to interact with Azure ML Studio and AWS SageMaker, and how to set up a Qlik tenant for AutoML. These steps are essential to get our environments ready for actual implementations.

Part 2:
Machine learning algorithms and models with Qlik

This section will cover the actual creation of machine learning project using Qlik tools with hands-on examples. The section starts with the setup process required to utilize the tools effectively. Techniques required to preprocess the data with Qlik Sense are covered in Chapter 6 followed by best practices for monitoring the models and handling the deployments. Towards the end of the section, we will cover the functionality of Qlik AutoML using concrete examples. At the end of this section, we will look at the important aspect of visualizing the results.

This section has the following chapters:

- *Chapter 5: Setting Up the Environments*
- *Chapter 6: Preprocessing and Exploring Data with Qlik Sense*
- *Chapter 7: Deploying and Monitoring Machine Learning Models*
- *Chapter 8: Utilising Qlik AutoML*
- *Chapter 9: Advanced Data Visualization Techniques for Machine Learning Solutions*

Setting Up the Environments

In previous chapters, we discovered some of the theories and frameworks behind machine learning problems. In this chapter, we will move toward practical implementation. Installing Qlik machine learning environments is an essential step in leveraging the power of machine learning within Qlik Sense. In this chapter, we will cover the process of installing and setting up various Qlik machine learning environments.

By the end of this chapter, we will have a solid understanding of the installation and configuration process for Qlik machine learning environments, allowing us to leverage the power of machine learning within Qlik Sense for data-driven decision making.

Here is what we will learn as part of this chapter:

- Advanced Analytics Integration with R and Python
- Setting up Qlik AutoML
- Cloud integrations with REST

Advanced Analytics Integration with R and Python

Advanced Analytics Integration is a feature that allows users to perform advanced data analysis and predictive modeling tasks within the Qlik Sense environment. With Advanced Analytics Integration, users can use popular statistical analysis and machine learning tools, such as R and Python, to build predictive models, perform data mining tasks, and gain insights from their data.

Data fetched from third-party systems using the Advanced Analytics connection is combined with data handled by the Qlik Associative Engine.

The workflow for Advanced Analytics Integration is illustrated in the following diagram:

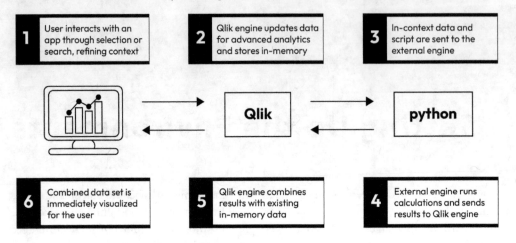

Figure 5.1: Advanced Analytics Integration workflow

Next, we will take a step-by-step look into the installation of R and Python integrations.

Installing Advanced Analytics Integration with R

In this section, we will install R with Advanced Analytics Integration in a Qlik Sense client-managed environment. Let's work through the following steps:

1. **Prerequisites**: You need the latest version of client-managed Qlik Sense installed and properly licensed (Server Side Extensions are supported since the Feb 2018 release of Qlik Sense). You should also have a user account with appropriate access rights to configure the connection in the **Qlik Management Console (QMC)**.

2. First, we need to download and install the R environment. It can be downloaded from `https://cloud.r-project.org/`.

   The base package of R is enough. At the time of writing, R-4.3.1 is the latest version but you should use the most recent one. The correct binary is determined by your given operating system. You can install R on the same server as the client-managed Qlik Sense instance or on a separate server. In this example, we will install R on the same server as Qlik Sense. You can proceed with the default settings in the installer.

3. Next, we will need to install the `Rserve` package on our R environment in order to extend R functionality to applications via TCP/IP. Rserve makes it possible to invoke R scripts remotely and the SSE bridge is utilizing it as a part of communication flow. Open the Windows command line and navigate to the `bin` folder of your R environment directory. You might need to run an elevated command prompt that requires administrator privileges. In our example, the command to navigate to the right directory is as follows:

```
cd C:\Program Files\R\R-4.3.0\bin
```

Once you are in the correct directory, open the R environment by typing R and pressing *Enter*. You should see a similar view to that shown in the following screenshot:

```
Rterm (64-bit)
Microsoft Windows [Version 10.0.17763.4010]
(c) 2018 Microsoft Corporation. All rights reserved.

C:\Users\qmi>cd C:\Program Files\R\R-4.3.0\bin

C:\Program Files\R\R-4.3.0\bin>R

R version 4.3.0 (2023-04-21 ucrt) -- "Already Tomorrow"
Copyright (C) 2023 The R Foundation for Statistical Computing
Platform: x86_64-w64-mingw32/x64 (64-bit)

R is free software and comes with ABSOLUTELY NO WARRANTY.
You are welcome to redistribute it under certain conditions.
Type 'license()' or 'licence()' for distribution details.

  Natural language support but running in an English locale

R is a collaborative project with many contributors.
Type 'contributors()' for more information and
'citation()' on how to cite R or R packages in publications.

Type 'demo()' for some demos, 'help()' for on-line help, or
'help.start()' for an HTML browser interface to help.
Type 'q()' to quit R.

>
```

Figure 5.2: R environment running on the command line

Type the following command to install the `Rserve` package:

```
install.packages('Rserve')
```

You might get a prompt asking you to select a CRAN mirror. Just select a location near you and press **OK**. `Rserve` is now installed on our environment. You can invoke it by typing the following commands:

```
library(Rserve)
Rserve()
```

You should see the following message stating that `Rserve` is now running and ready for commands:

```
> Rserve: Ok, ready to answer queries.
```

4. We need a bridge component between Rserve and Qlik Sense. Qlik provides an open source plugin version of this bridge component for R, which we will use in this example. There is also the possibility of developing your own bridge. Download the bridge from the following URL: `https://github.com/qlik-oss/sse-r-plugin`.

> **Note**
>
> The plugin is written using C# and by default must be built. There is a prebuilt version of the plugin available in the `releases` section of the repository: `https://github.com/qlik-oss/sse-r-plugin/releases/tag/v1.2.1`.
>
> In this example, we will use the newest prebuilt version since compiling C# source code is out of the scope of this book. The **Bridge** component is used to provide the interface between the Qlik Advanced Analytics connector and third-party analytics engine. It is based on Google Remote Procedure Calls.

Once you have either built the package or downloaded the prebuilt version, open a new command line, navigate to the folder containing `SSEtoRserve.exe`, and launch it from the command line. The following view should appear:

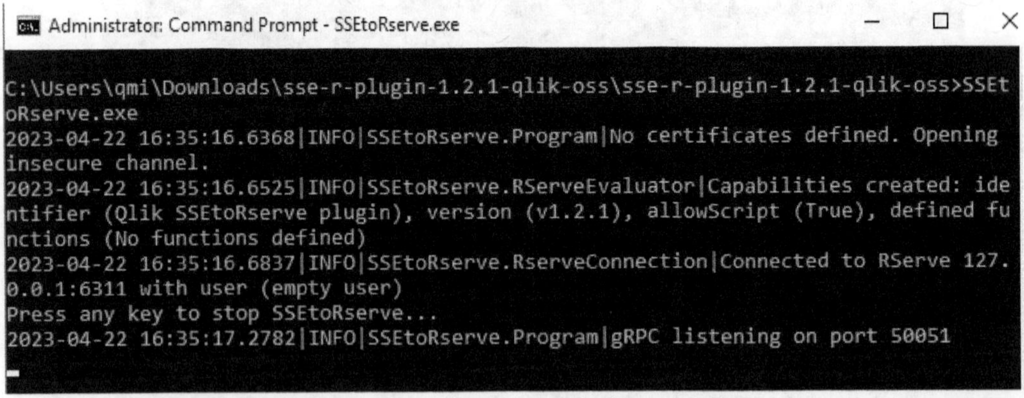

Figure 5.3: SSEtoRserve running on the command line

We have now verified that the bridge component can connect to Rserve. You should now close all open command-line windows before moving to the next step!

> **Note**
>
> The bridge component can run on the same server as the Qlik Sense environment or R environment, or on a separate server. Typically, it is recommended to install the bridge on the same server as Qlik Sense. In this example, we will install all the components on the same server.
>
> If the bridge component and R environment are on different servers, you have to configure the bridge component to connect to the correct IP address and port where Rserve is running. To do that, modify the values in the `SSEtoRserve.exe.config` file in the same directory as `SSEtoRserve.exe`. There are also other options in this file, including settings for certificates, among other things.

5. Next, we will set up both R and our SSE-to-R bridge to run as a service. This will allow us to have an environment up and running all the time without the need to manually restart the services from the command line. There are multiple tools that can be used to run command-line scripts and programs as a service. In this example, we will use a free tool called NSSM. NSSM makes it easier to install and manage Windows services. Let's start by downloading NSSM from the following link: `https://nssm.cc/download`.

Once you have finished downloading NSSM, extract the files from the `.zip` package and navigate to the `win64` folder (or `win32` if you are using a 32-bit environment) found inside the extracted folder using the command line. Make sure that you are running the command line with admin privileges.

We will start by installing Rserve as a service. To launch NSSM, type the following command:

```
nssm install RserveService
```

You should see a small window open, as shown in the following figure. Next, we will configure our Rserve instance to run as a service. The **Path** field needs to point to the `Rserve.exe` file that can be found among the libraries in our R installation folder. An example path is the following:

```
C:\Program Files\R\R-4.3.0\library\Rserve\libs\x64\Rserve.exe
```

The **Startup directory** field should point to the directory where `Rserve.exe` is located. An example of these settings is shown in the following screenshot:

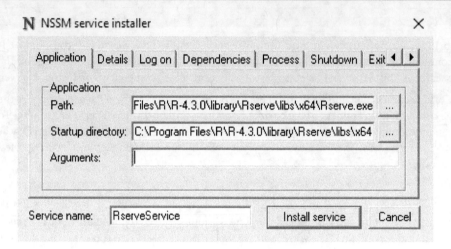

Figure 5.4: NSSM Rserve setup

Press the **Install service** button and you should get a message stating that the service was installed successfully.

To successfully run our Rserve service, we need to define the path to our R environment in the environment variables. To do that, let's first open the environment variables window. It can be found by launching **Control Panel → System and Security → System** and selecting **Advanced system settings** on the left. The **System Properties** window will open. Click the **Environment Variables** button at the bottom of the window.

The **Environment Variables** window will open and, at the bottom part of the window, you should see **System variables**. Find the variable called Path and activate that. Then, press the **Edit** button. The **Edit environment variable** window opens.

Select **New** on the right side of the window and type the correct path to the directory containing your R executable. An example path is the following (You should use the actual path of your R installation here):

```
C:\Program Files\R\R-4.3.0\bin\x64
```

Confirm the edit by pressing **OK**. We also need to configure the R_HOME environment variable. For that, select **New** under **System variables**. Insert R_HOME into the **Variable name** field and add the path to the R environment root folder into the **Variable value** field.

The following screenshot shows an example:

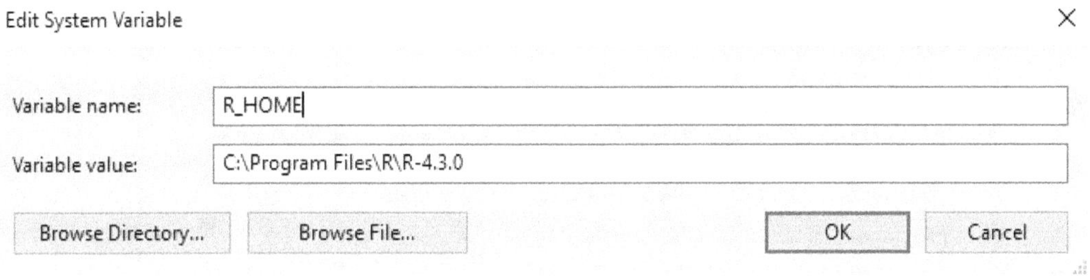

Figure 5.5: System variable example

Press **OK** on all three windows until you get back to **Control Panel**. The system variables have now been created.

Next, we will install the bridge component as a service. Start by typing the following command into the same command-line window that we used in the previous step:

```
nssm install SSEtoRServe
```

A similar setup window to the one we saw in an earlier step should appear. Here, we will set our path to point to our SSEtoRServe.exe file located in our bridge connector folder. An example path is the following:

```
C:\Users\qmi\Downloads\sse-r-plugin-1.2.1-qlik-oss\sse-r-plugin-
1.2.1-qlik-oss\SSEtoRserve.exe
```

The setup should look similar to the following screenshot:

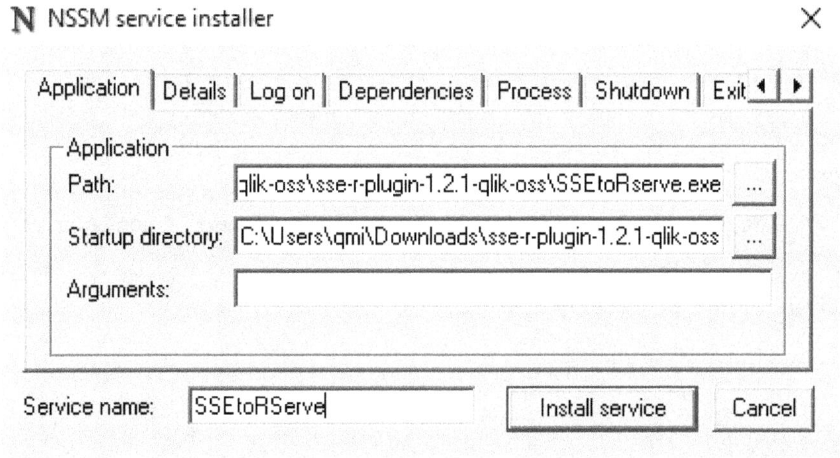

Figure 5.6: NSSM SSEtoRserve setup

Next, we will set `RserveService` as a dependency for our `SSEtoRServe` service. To do that, open the **Dependencies** tab and type `RserveService` into the window, as follows:

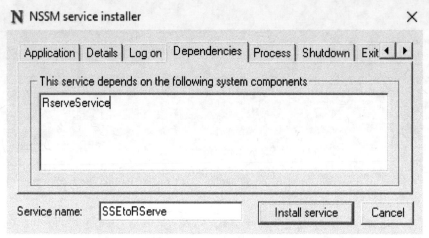

Figure 5.7: SSEtoRServe dependencies configuration

After pressing the **Install service** button, we should get confirmation of a successful installation.

Next, we can open the **Services** view from Windows and start our **SSEtoRserve** service. That should also fire up **RserveService**. Verify that both services are running correctly before proceeding to the next step.

6. The next step is to configure the Advanced Analytics connection in the QMC. Open **QMC** and navigate to the **Analytic Connections** section. Select **Create New**. The **Edit analytic connection** view will open. Insert the following parameters and press **Apply**:

- **Name**: R
- **Host**: localhost
- **Port**: 50051
- **Certificate file path**: Leave empty at this point. This can be used to configure a certificate for the connection.
- **Reconnect timeout (seconds)**: 20
- **Request timeout (seconds)**: 0

An example of the settings is shown in the following screenshot:

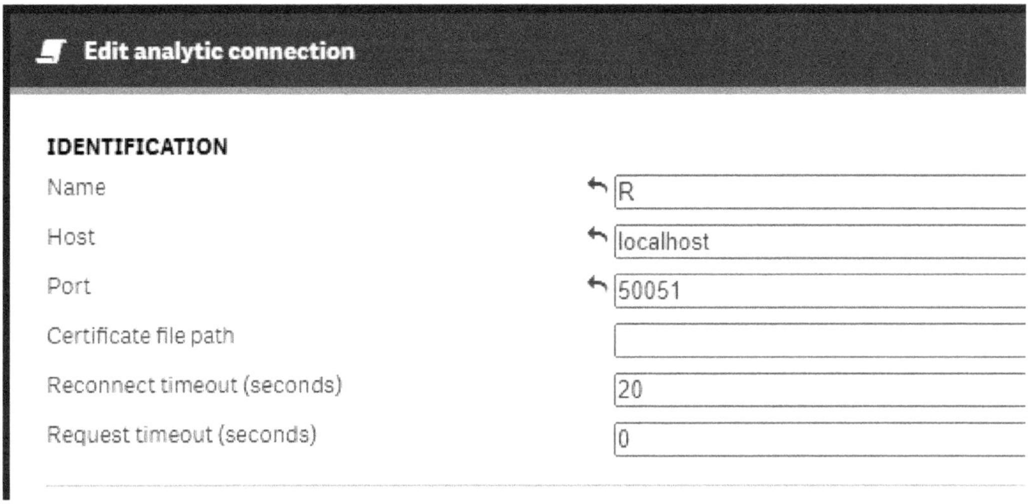

Edit analytic connection

IDENTIFICATION

Name	R
Host	localhost
Port	50051
Certificate file path	
Reconnect timeout (seconds)	20
Request timeout (seconds)	0

Figure 5.8: Analytic connection settings in the QMC

7. Next, we can test that our connection works correctly. Open any Qlik Sense application or create a new one with some dummy data. Add a new sheet in the application and drag a KPI object onto the canvas.

Insert the following formula into the expression field in the KPI object:

```
R.ScriptEval('1+2')
```

The first part of the script tells the engine to utilize our newly created analytics connection. You can reference any analytics connection using its name as defined in the QMC. In this case, the name of our connection is R. The second part is a function provided by our bridge plugin. There are eight functions provided in total. We will take a deeper look at how to utilize these in *Chapter 7*. In this test, we will send a simple formula to sum two numbers in the R environment. R returns the sum of our calculation, and we should see it displayed in the KPI object:

R.ScriptEval('1+2')

3

Figure 5.9: Example of a KPI calculated in R

We have now verified that our environment is working correctly. You can utilize the connection from the load script during data loads or on the fly just as we did with our example KPI.

> **Note**
>
> The `SSEtoRserve` component writes a log into the `/logs` folder located in the `root` folder of the bridge. That log is a good place to start debugging possible issues and monitoring the performance of the environment and the models.

> **Note**
>
> If you want to run the Advanced Analytics connection on a Qlik Sense Desktop instance, you can add the connection details to the `Settings.ini` file located under `Documents/Qlik/Sense`. To create a connection to the R environment, add the following line:
>
> `SSEPlugin=R,localhost:50051`
>
> Remember to add an empty line at the end of the file and then save it. Your Qlik Sense Desktop instance should now be able to connect to R using the Advanced Analytics connection. (Note that the `SSEtoRserve` bridge and Rserve must be running on your computer before starting Qlik Sense Desktop.)

Installing Advanced Analytics Integration with Python

We can also utilize Python with the Advanced Analytics connection. In this section, we will install Python with Advanced Analytics Integration in a client-managed Qlik Sense environment. Let's do this with the following steps:

1. **Prerequisites**: You need the latest version of client-managed Qlik Sense installed and properly licensed. You should also have a user account with appropriate access rights to configure the connection in the QMC.

2. Download and install Python: `https://www.python.org/downloads/`.

   When the installer launches, select **Add python.exe to PATH** and press **Install Now**.

This phase of the installer can be seen in the following screenshot:

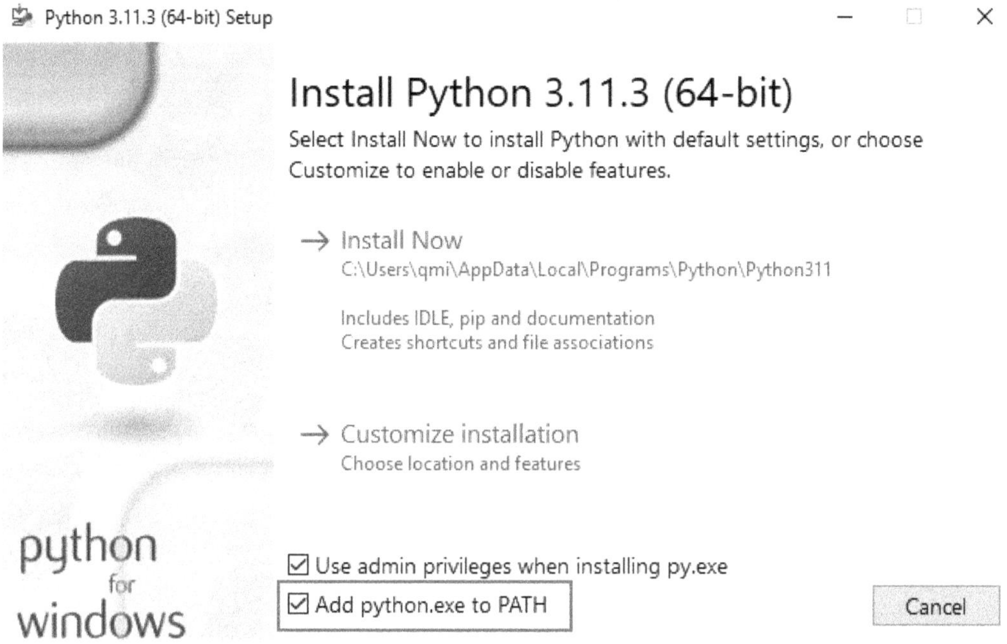

Figure 5.10: Python installation settings

3. After Python is successfully installed, we will add some libraries to it. Here, we are installing some of the most common statistical libraries needed in order to communicate through the bridge component. You can also install additional libraries based on your needs. Open a new command-line window and type the following commands:

```
python -m pip install --upgrade pip
python -m pip install grpcio
python -m pip install numpy
python -m pip install nose
python -m pip install google
python -m pip install protobuf==3.20.*
```

4. For this example, we will also use predefined bridge that is created by Qlik. Download it from https://github.com/qlik-oss/server-side-extension/releases/tag/v1.1.0 and extract it to the server.

5. Next, we will configure our analytics connection in the QMC. Open **QMC** and select **Analytics connection**. Insert the following values:

    * **Name**: `Script`

    * **Host**: `localhost`

    * **Port**: `50051`

    * **Certificate file path**: Leave empty at this point. This can be used to configure a certificate for the connection.

    * **Reconnect timeout (seconds)**: `20`

    * **Request timeout (seconds)**: `0`

6. Next, we will import our example application. Navigate to the folder containing the bridge downloaded in *step 4*. From there, navigate to the `\examples\python\FullScriptSupport` folder and look for an application called `SSE_Full_Script_Support.qvf`. Import that into your Qlik Sense environment.

7. Open the command line and navigate to the folder containing the bridge downloaded in *step 4*. From there, navigate to the `\examples\python\FullScriptSupport` folder. Type the following command and press *Enter*:

    ```
    python ExtensionService_Script.py
    ```

    You should see the following lines in a command-line window:

    ```
    2023-04-23 13:29:19,950 — INFO — Logging enabled
    2023-04-23 13:29:19,966 — INFO - *** Running server in insecure
    mode on port: 50051 ***
    ```

    The Python environment is now running and ready to take commands from the Qlik application.

> **Note**
>
> If you are installing this example on the same environment as the previous R example, you need to change the port for this Python example. To do that, you can modify the code in the `ExtensionService_Script.py` file located in the same folder where we ran our example in *step 7*. The port is defined on line *117*:
>
> `parser.add_argument('—port', nargs='?', default='50051')`
>
> Change that and make the corresponding change in **QMC → Analytic connection**.

> **Note**
>
> You can also set up a Python environment to run as a service using the same method described earlier with R components. We will not cover that part in detail here, but basically, you can install Python as a service using NSSM and give the script as an argument.

8. Open the `SSE_Full_Script_Support.qvf` file that we imported in *step 6* to verify the functionality. If you open the first sheet of the application, you should see the following:

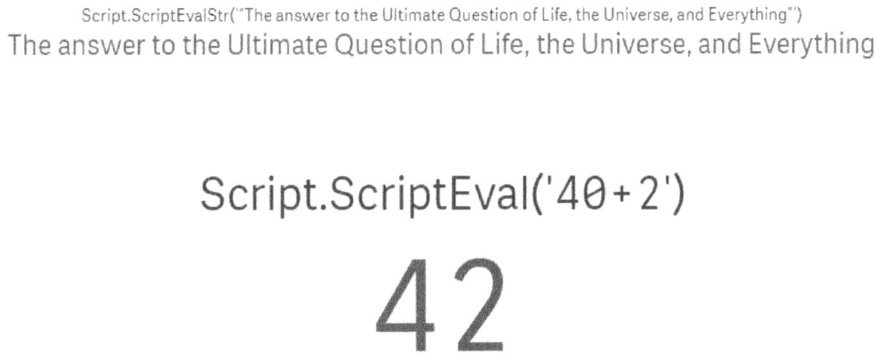

Script.ScriptEvalStr("The answer to the Ultimate Question of Life, the Universe, and Everything")
The answer to the Ultimate Question of Life, the Universe, and Everything

Script.ScriptEval('40+2')

42

Figure 5.11: Python connection working

We have now successfully installed Python with the Advanced Analytics connection on Qlik.

Setting up Qlik AutoML

Since Qlik AutoML is a SaaS solution, there is minimal setup required. In this section, we will look at the necessary steps to utilize AutoML. We will assume that a Qlik Cloud tenant is up and running. The Basic tier of Qlik AutoML is included as part of the Qlik Cloud subscription license. We will take a deep dive into Qlik AutoML itself in *Chapter 8*. To prepare our environment for that chapter, the following steps are needed:

1. Navigate to **Management Console** in Qlik Cloud and open the **Settings** tab.

2. Under the **Feature control** section, make sure that **Machine learning endpoints** is enabled, as seen in the following screenshot:

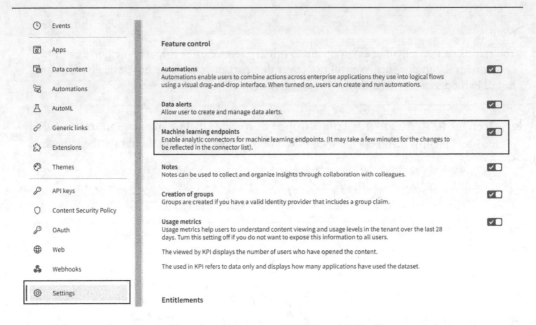

Figure 5.12: Machine learning endpoints setting

3. Select **Analytics Services** and create a shared space called `ML experiments`. This will be our space for all the work done in *Chapter 8*.

Our cloud environment is now set up and ready. We will now explore various integrations that we can use with Qlik Cloud.

Cloud integrations with REST

There are many third-party machine learning and AI platforms on the market. You can connect to most of these from Qlik Cloud. In this section, we will briefly look at the different options and requirements for each connection. We will not create the actual models on top of third-party tools in this chapter.

To start using connections to third-party machine learning endpoints, you must enable them from **Management Console** in Qlik Cloud. If you have been following this chapter from the beginning, we completed that step in the previous section.

There are dedicated connectors available for the most common machine learning tools out there. At the time of writing this book, the connectors are as follows:

- The general Advanced Analytics connector
- Amazon Comprehend connector

- Amazon SageMaker connector

- Azure ML connector

- Azure OpenAI connector

- Databricks MLflow connector

- DataRobot connector

- Qlik AutoML connector

- Qlik GeoOperations connector

- OpenAI connector

All these connections are available when you select **Add New** → **Data connection** in Qlik Cloud. Analytics connections can send data to external machine learning endpoints for calculation. The functionality is similar to what we discovered with the R and Python connections earlier in this chapter. The data connection can be utilized either from a load script or *on the fly* from visualization expressions. We will go deeper into the syntax in *Chapter 7*.

Let's take a closer look at some of these connectors.

General Advanced Analytics connector

To use a generic connector, there must be an endpoint to connect to, and this endpoint must be publicly accessible by the Qlik Cloud environment. The parameters for these connections are the following:

- **URL**: Host URL for the platform where the model is deployed.

- **Method**: GET or POST.

- **Content Type**: Content type for the request header. For example, `application/json`.

- **HTTP Headers**: Custom headers sent with each request.

- **Query Parameters**: Parameters that will be attached to the end of the URL.

- **Authorization Method**: None, Bearer Token, or AWS Auth v4 Signature.

- **Request**: Format and content of the request.

- **Response Fields**: Whether to load all fields. If this is not selected, you can specify the fields to be loaded.

- **Response Table**: Definition of specific table fields. If the previous parameter is not checked, this is used to determine the fields to be loaded.

- **Association**: A field containing a unique identifier. The result table will be associated with the source table using this information. This can be any field containing a unique ID.

- **Name**: Connection name.

Once you create a connection, it will appear under **Data connections** in **Data load editor**.

Amazon SageMaker connector

Amazon SageMaker is a well-known machine learning platform. There is a dedicated connector to interact with SageMaker from Qlik Cloud. To connect to a SageMaker endpoint, it must be publicly accessible by Qlik Cloud. The parameters for this connector are the following:

- **Endpoint Name**: Identifier used by the endpoint in the AWS environment.

- **Model Name**: Name given for the deployed model in AWS.

- **Model Variant Name**: If a multi-model endpoint is deployed, this parameter is used to recognize the variant. For a simple endpoint, this should not be provided.

- **Settings**: **Region** is where the AWS Region for the service is specified, and **Use FIPS Endpoint** specifies whether there is a need for a FIPS-compliant endpoint.

- **Authentication**: Here we use the AWS access key and secret key found in the AWS console.

- **Response Format**: JSON or Text Array. Most models use JSON.

- **Response Table**: **Name of Returned Table** identifies the table returned by the model and **Table Path** can be used to specify the table using a JMES path.

- **Response Fields**: Whether to load all fields. If this is not selected, you can specify the fields to be loaded using the **Table Fields** selector.

- **Association**: A field containing a unique identifier. The result table will be associated with the source table using this information. This can be any field with a unique ID.

- **Name**: Connection name.

Azure ML connector

Azure ML is another well-known machine learning platform. To connect to an Azure ML endpoint, it must be publicly accessible by Qlik Cloud. These are the parameters for this connector:

- **Format**: Azure ML or Azure ML (Legacy). Legacy format should be used for models created before January 2022.

- **Endpoint Name**: Identifier used for the endpoint in Azure.

- **Authentication**: The Azure ML Endpoint Key obtained from the Azure portal.

- **Request**: **Web Service Input Name** is the name of the JSON object expected by the model.

- **Response Table**: Here, **Name of Returned Table** identifies the table returned by the model and **Table Path** can be used to specify the table using the JMES path.

- **Response Fields**: Whether to load all fields. If this is not selected, you can specify the fields to be loaded using the **Table Fields** selector.

- **Association**: A field containing a unique identifier. The result table will be associated with the source table using this information. This can be any field with a unique ID.

- **Name**: Connection name.

Qlik AutoML connector

Qlik AutoML is a machine learning environment in Qlik Cloud and has its own dedicated connection. We will take a closer look at AutoML and how to use it in *Chapter 8*. The parameters for Qlik AutoML connector are as follows:

- **Connection**: Name of the deployed ML model.

- **Response Table**: **Name of the Returned Table** is the table returned by the model. You can also specify whether you would like to include SHAP values, the source dataset, and any errors in the response.

- **Association**: A field containing a unique identifier. The result table will be associated with the source table using this information. This can be any field with a unique ID.

- **Name**: Connection name.

We have now looked briefly at some of the parameters required by Advanced Analytics connections from Qlik Cloud to both third-party machine learning environments and Qlik AutoML. We will utilize some of these endpoints in later parts of this book.

> **Note**
>
> An interesting part of the analytics connector package are the OpenAI connector and Azure OpenAI connector. These connectors will provide a seamless integration into generative AI models. The principles of the connection are similar to the other analytics connections but there are an endless number of possibilities. In this chapter, we are not going deeper into setting up a connection, but you can find detailed instructions in the Qlik help site.

Summary

In this chapter, we started to move toward the practical implementation of machine learning models with Qlik. To prepare for the coming chapters, we installed different environments.

First, we went through the installation of the R environment and the Advanced Analytics connection from a client-managed Qlik Sense instance in R. We covered the steps to run the components as a service and created a simple sample application to verify the functionality.

We also installed a Python environment and connected that to our Qlik environment using Advanced Analytics Integration. We demonstrated the functionality of this environment using an example application. At the end of this chapter, we moved from on-premises into cloud environments and discovered how to create connections to external AI and machine learning platforms using REST. We also did a few setup steps for our AutoML environment to get it ready for our coming chapters.

In the next chapter, we will investigate the data-modeling capabilities of Qlik Sense. We will learn how to create a data model, how to clean data, and how to analyze it. We will learn about different techniques and tools to be able to prepare a perfect dataset for our machine learning purposes. We will utilize the skills learned here throughout the next chapter when we start to implement and create actual machine learning models.

6

Preprocessing and Exploring Data with Qlik Sense

Data processing and exploration are essential steps in the data analysis process. They involve transforming raw data into meaningful insights, identifying patterns, and gaining a deeper understanding of the data. Qlik Sense is a powerful data analytics tool that allows users to easily process and explore data. With its data cleansing, transformation, and integration capabilities, Qlik Sense makes it easy to prepare data for analysis and produce a good dataset to be used for machine learning models.

This chapter will introduce data preprocessing and exploration with Qlik Sense. We will cover the following main topics:

- Creating a data model using the data manager
- Creating a data model and altering data with Qlik script
- Validating data
- Utilizing data lineage and data catalogs
- Exploring data and finding insights using Insight Advisor

Creating a data model with the data manager

A good data model is important because it forms the foundation of effective data analysis. A data model is a representation of the structure and relationships within a dataset, and it defines the rules for how data is stored, accessed, and used.

Qlik's data manager is a data preparation and management tool that is part of the Qlik Sense platform. It provides a user-friendly interface for designing and building data models, as well as cleaning, transforming, and integrating data from a variety of sources.

Qlik's data manager provides a range of features to support data preparation and management, including the following:

- **Data profiling**: Qlik's data manager provides tools that help users understand their data, including data profiling features, which allow users to identify data quality issues, such as missing values, duplicates, and outliers.

- **Data transformation**: Qlik's data manager provides a range of tools for cleaning and transforming data, including the ability to remove duplicates, fill in missing values, and convert data types. It also provides advanced transformation capabilities, such as data pivoting and data normalization.

- **Data integration**: Qlik's data manager allows users to integrate data from a variety of sources, including Excel spreadsheets, CSV files, databases, and cloud-based services. It provides built-in connectors to popular data sources and the ability to create custom connectors for other data sources.

- **Data modeling**: Qlik's data manager allows users to create data models using a graphical interface. It provides tools for defining tables, fields, and relationships between tables, as well as the ability to add calculated fields and build complex data models.

Next, we will look into these features of the data manager using an example dataset. We will not cover a full data model creation in detail since that is not in within the scope of this book.

> **Note**
> The example dataset used in these examples can be found from the GitHub repository of this book.

Introduction to the data manager

Let's start getting familiar with the data manager by taking a look at the user interface. As a preparation step we have created a new analytics application in the Qlik cloud tenant and uploaded our sample dataset (`Sales Multi Table.xlsx`). The data manager view will open. An example of that view can be seen in the following figure:

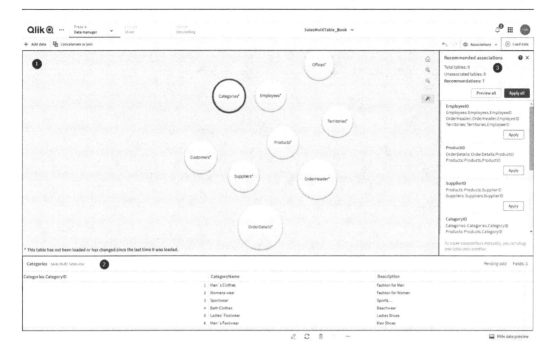

Figure 6.1: The data manager view

In this figure, we have divided the data manager into three different sections, which we will cover next:

1. **Data modeling**: In this space you can create the actual data model. One bubble represents the entity of data, for example, an Excel sheet or database table. When clicking the left mouse button on a bubble, the color of other bubbles will change. This color represents how well these two entities link with each other.

2. **Data preview**: If you have activated one data entity or bubble, the data preview shows the snapshot of all the columns and sample data about the entity. The active entity is highlighted with darker borders in the data modeling view. You can enter the data edit view, refresh, and delete data entities from this view.

3. **Associations**: All associations between the entities that are discovered by the data manager can be seen on the right side of the screen. You can preview the associations and approve these using this view.

Next, we will take a look at how to create a data model using our sample dataset. We will start by dragging a data entity called **Categories** on top of the data entity called **Products**. When we start dragging the **Categories** entity, we will see a view similar to the following:

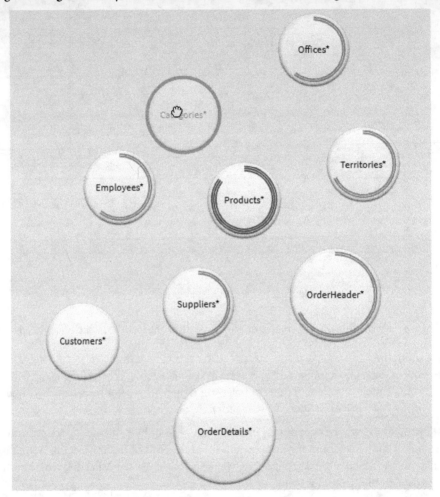

Figure 6.2: Data manager – linking tables together

In this picture, we see that **Products** entity has a green arc on the outer edge and several other entities have an orange arc. The arc and color represent the match between the two entities. Since the **Products** entity is the best match, we can drop our **Categories** entity on top of **Products**. We have now linked these two data entities together. The actual linking table is visible at the bottom of the data modeling view. It is highlighted in the following figure:

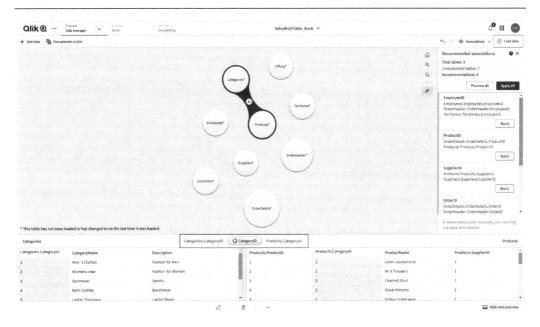

Figure 6.3: The data manager – association done

If you'd like to edit the linking field, that can be done by pressing the button in the middle of the highlighted area. You can now proceed to building the rest of the data model. This can be done either one by one or by selecting **Apply all** button located at the top section of the **Associations** view, as seen in the following figure:

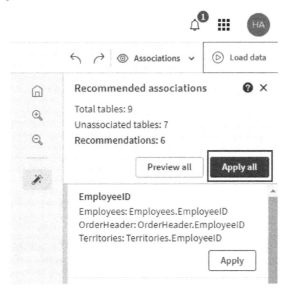

Figure 6.4: The Apply all button

You should see the ready data model. It should look like the one in the following figure:

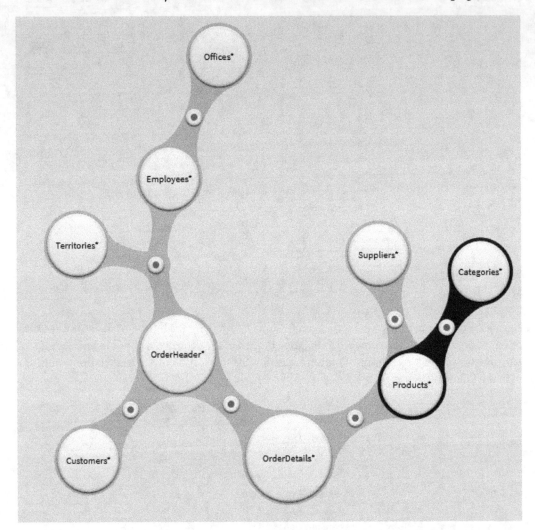

Figure 6.5: Data model ready

Next, we will take a closer look into editing capabilities in the data manager. We will start by selecting the **Employees** entity. We should see the content of **Employees** in the **Data preview** section.

To modify the entity, we will select the small pen icon located at the bottom of the **Data preview** section. The **Data edit** view will open and should look like the one in the following figure:

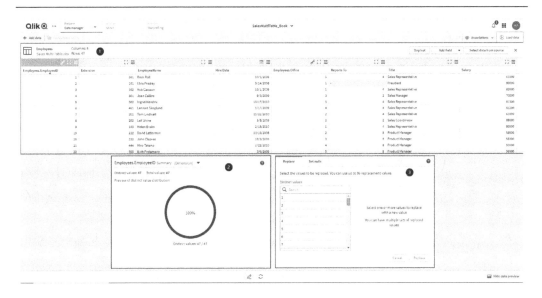

Figure 6.6: The Data edit view

The Data edit view is divided into the following sections:

1. **Data preview**: This is a preview of the data entity that has been opened for editing. You can also see the data types that are auto-detected on top of each column. For example, datetime fields and fields containing geo-based data are marked and handled accordingly. An auto-calendar is created for `datetime` fields, and coordinates are assigned to geodata.

2. **Data summary**: The data summary will show statistics and the distribution of the data. This section is good for validation and outlier detection. This section will also tell you how many total values and unique values there are in an specific column.

3. **Data editing**: The data editing section will allow you to perform several operations on the data field using graphical tools. These operations contain null value replacements, replacing certain values with others, creating buckets and splitting data. For example, null value replacement is an important preprocessing step for machine learning.

Next, we will take a closer look into some of the sections using the **Employees** entity as an example. Let's select the **Salary** column and change its type to **Measure** in the **Summary** section. You should see something like the following figure:

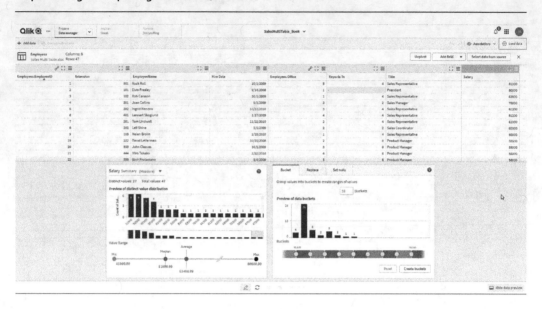

Figure 6.7: The Salary field active in the Data edit view

We can see that the data preview section shows us the minimum, median, average, and maximum values and the distribution of each individual value. The data editing section will give us options to create for example data buckets, replace certain values, and set values to null fields.

Let's next activate the **EmployeeName** field. We will see the following view, which will differ slightly from the one we saw for the **Salary** field:

Figure 6.8: The EmployeeName field active in the Data edit view

Now we can see a different view in the data summary section that shows the unique values and total values. We will also see new options in our data edit section. There is an option to split the field, for example, into first name and last name, and you can also set the order. We don't see an option for buckets with this field since **EmployeeName** is a text field.

In the upper right corner, we can see the **Add field** button and under that, we can add a calculated field. If we select that, a wizard guiding us on field creation will appear. Let's create a calculated field for our **Employee** entity. A wizard, as shown in the following figure, should be visible:

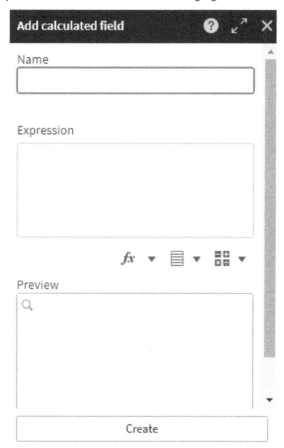

Figure 6.9: Add calculated field

In this case, we would like to calculate our employee's monthly salary within two decimals. We will name our field MontlySalary and give the following expression in the **Expression** field:

```
Round((Salary/12),0.01)
```

The **Preview** section will show the sample values while we are typing our calculation. You can access fields, functions, and operators using the buttons under the **Expression** section. When ready, press **Create** to add the calculated field to our data entity.

When you look into the header section of each field, you can see the icons highlighted in the following figure:

Figure 6.10: Headers in the Data edit view

The icon on the left side will give you the option to change the data type of each field. The data manager should automatically recognize most of the data fields. For example, in the previous image, the **Hire Date** field is recognized as a `Date` type and there is a small calendar icon, while other fields are of the generic type. Available field types are **General**, **Date**, **Timestamp**, and **Geodata**.

Fields that have associations are marked with a chain icon, as seen in the previous figure, on top of the `Employees.EmployeeID` field and the `Employees.Office` field. You can edit or break the association by selecting the chain icon.

The right-most icon will give you options to modify the field. Under that, you can find options to rename the field, associate the field with other tables, edit sorting, hide the field from analysis, and view details.

We have now gone briefly through most of the features in the data manager. The next step is to load data into Qlik's engine. To do that, we can select the **Load data** button located in the top-right corner. Data loading will start and after that, we can move on to the visualization part.

In the next section, we will take a brief look into Qlik script. We will discover some of the most important functions that we can utilize in our machine learning and data visualization solutions.

> **Note**
> The data manager generates Qlik script in the background. A good way to start investigating scripting is to create a data model using the data manager and switch to the data load editor to see the generated script.

> **Note**
>
> A data model can be viewed using the data model viewer. The data model viewer will represent the relationships between tables and give a sample of the data that each table contains. We will not cover the usage in depth in this book.

Introduction to Qlik script

Qlik script is a scripting language used in Qlik Sense and QlikView for loading and transforming data from various sources into Qlik's associative data model. It is a powerful and flexible scripting language that allows users to extract, transform, and load data from various sources, such as databases, spreadsheets, and flat files, and then prepare that data for analysis.

Qlik script is like SQL in terms of syntax and structure, but it includes additional features and functions that make it more powerful and flexible. With Qlik script, users can perform complex data transformations, create calculated fields, generate variables, and apply filters to data. The script can be used to define data models, specify data sources, and load data from them, and define data transformations. The data manager that we used in the previous section generates Qlik script in the background, and all operations done using the data manager can be done using scripting.

When using Qlik script, the following procedures are typically involved in creating a data model for an application:

1. **Connect to a data source**: First, we need to establish a connection to a data source. This could be a database, Excel file, CSV file, or any other supported data format. Creating data connections is not covered in detail in this book.

2. **Start the script**: We will begin by writing a script statement to initiate the script. In Qlik, a script typically starts with the LOAD keyword.

3. **Load data from the data source**: Use the LOAD statement to fetch data from your data source into Qlik. Specify the fields you want to load and the source table or file. In this example, we will load the Employees table and Office table from Sales Multi Table.xlsx. These tables will link through the [Office] field since, in Qlik script, fields with similar names will form a link. You can modify the name using the as keyword.

    ```
    [Employees]:
    LOAD
            [EmployeeID],
            [Extension],
            [EmployeeName],
            [Hire Date],
            [Office],
            [Reports To],
            [Title],
    ```

```
        [Year Salary] AS [Salary]
 FROM [lib://DataFiles/Sales Multi Table.xlsx]
(ooxml, embedded labels, table is Employees);
[Offices]:
LOAD
        [Office],
        [SalesOffice],
        APPLYMAP( '__cityKey2GeoPoint', APPLYMAP( '__cityName2Key',
LOWER([SalesOffice]) ), '-') AS [Offices.SalesOffice_GeoInfo]
 FROM [lib://DataFiles/Sales Multi Table.xlsx]
(ooxml, embedded labels, table is Offices);
```

4. **Transform and clean the data**: Perform any necessary transformations or cleaning operations on the loaded data. This may include renaming fields, changing data types, filtering rows, or joining tables. Qlik provides various functions and operators to manipulate data. We will take a closer look into some of the functions in the next section.

5. **Create table associations**: Qlik's associative data model allows you to establish relationships between tables based on common fields. You can also create joins between tables and concatenate data if needed.

6. **Save and reload the script**: After completing the script, save it and click the reload button. This will load the data into the Qlik application and create the data model.

Important functions in Qlik script

In this section, we will take a closer look into some of the functions in Qlik script that are helpful when creating a machine learning-ready data model:

- **Date functions**: Qlik provides a variety of date functions, such as Date(), Year(), Month(), Day(), and Quarter(), to extract and manipulate date-related information from fields.

- **String functions**: Qlik offers numerous string functions, such as Len(), Upper(), Lower(), Concatenate(), Left(), Right(), Mid(), and SubField(), for string manipulation and formatting.

  This is an example using the Upper() function:

```
LOAD
    CustomerID,
    Upper(CustomerName) AS CustomerName
FROM
    [Customers.csv];
```

- **Numeric functions**: Qlik provides various numeric functions, such as `Sum()`, `Avg()`, `Min()`, `Max()`, `Count()`, `Round()`, `Ceil()`, `Floor()`, and `Abs()` for performing calculations and aggregations. These functions are useful when preparing data for machine learning.

  This is an example using the `Sum()` function:

  ```
  LOAD
      CustomerID,
      Sum(SalesAmount) AS TotalSales
  FROM
      [Sales.csv]
  GROUP BY
      CustomerID;
  ```

- **AGGR**: The AGGR function is used to aggregate data dynamically based on user-defined expressions. It allows you to perform calculations at different levels of granularity.

  This is an example:

  ```
  Sales:
  LOAD
      Product,
      Category,
      Price,
      Quantity
  FROM
      [Sales.csv];
  CategorySales:
  LOAD
      Category,
      AGGR(Sum(Price * Quantity), Category) AS TotalSales
  RESIDENT
      Sales
  GROUP BY
      Category;
  ```

  In this example, we have a dataset of sales transactions (`Sales`). We want to calculate the total sales for each category by summing the product of price and quantity for each transaction.

- **IF-THEN-ELSE**: The IF-THEN-ELSE statement is used to perform conditional logic. It allows you to create conditional expressions and perform different actions based on the condition.

  This is an example:

  ```
  Sales:
  LOAD
      Product,
      Category,
      Price,
      If(Category = 'Electronics', Price * 0.9, Price) AS
  DiscountedPrice
  FROM
      [Sales.csv];
  ```

  In this example, if the `Category` field is equal to `Electronics`, the `DiscountedPrice` field will be calculated as 90% of the original price (`Price * 0.9`). Otherwise, if `Category` is not `Electronics`, the `DiscountedPrice` field will be the same as the original price (`Price`).

- **Loops**: There are the looping structures in Qlik script that will help you to perform more complex operations:

  - **FOR...NEXT**: The `FOR...NEXT` loop allows you to execute a block of script code for a specified number of iterations. It's typically used when you know the exact number of iterations in advance.

  - **DO...WHILE**: The `DO...WHILE` loop executes a block of code repeatedly as long as a condition is true. It's useful when you want to iterate until a specific condition is met.

  - **FOR EACH...NEXT**: The `FOR EACH...NEXT` loop allows you to iterate over the distinct values of a field or expression. It executes a block of code for each unique value.

  - **WHILE...WEND**: The `WHILE...WEND` loop repeatedly executes a block of code as long as a condition is true. It's useful when you want to iterate until a specific condition becomes false.

- Other useful functions that might be handy when modeling data for machine learning are listed here:

  - **APPLYMAP**: The `APPLYMAP` function allows you to perform mapping operations by referencing an external mapping table. This can be useful for mapping categorical values to numerical codes or vice versa, which is often required in machine learning tasks.

  - **RESIDENT**: The `RESIDENT` function allows you to perform operations on a previously loaded table. It is useful for creating derived tables or applying transformations to existing data, which can be beneficial for preparing data for machine learning algorithms.

- **PIVOT** and **UNPIVOT**: The PIVOT and UNPIVOT functions enable you to reshape your data, converting it between wide and long formats. This functionality can be valuable for feature engineering and data preprocessing in machine learning workflows.

- **CONCATENATE**: The CONCATENATE function allows you to combine multiple tables with the same structure into a single table. This can be handy for aggregating data from different sources or merging datasets, which is often necessary for machine learning tasks.

- **LOAD INLINE**: The LOAD INLINE statement allows you to define data inline within your script. This is useful when you have small datasets or need to define example data for testing machine learning algorithms.

- **PRECEDING LOAD**: The PRECEDING LOAD feature enables you to calculate and store derived fields within the load script. It allows you to perform calculations and transformations on the fly, which can be advantageous for feature engineering or creating target variables for machine learning models.

- **APPLY** and **GROUP BY APPLY**: The APPLY and GROUP BY APPLY functions allow you to perform advanced calculations and transformations on groups of data. They provide a way to apply complex expressions and aggregations within a group, which can be beneficial for creating features or generating summary statistics for machine learning algorithms.

- **QUALIFY** and **UNQUALIFY**: The QUALIFY and UNQUALIFY functions are used to specify field qualifiers. They are particularly helpful when working with fields that contain characters that have special meaning in Qlik scripting, such as spaces or special characters, which are commonly encountered in feature names or labels in machine learning tasks.

> **Note**
> A full Qlik script reference guide with examples is available at the Qlik help site.

Now we have taken a brief overview of some of the most important functions in Qlik script. Qlik scripting is a powerful tool for manipulating data and creating data models. Next, we will take a closer look into data validation using multiple tools in Qlik Cloud.

Validating data

We have multiple options to validate and investigate our data with Qlik Cloud before moving to the data editing and analysis phase. Let's start by using a data catalog. We will take a closer look into data catalogs in the next section of this chapter, but in this section, we will cover some of the features for data validation. First, we will open Sales Multi table.xlsx and move to the **Fields** section in our data catalog. Let's also select the **Employees** tab. We should see the following view:

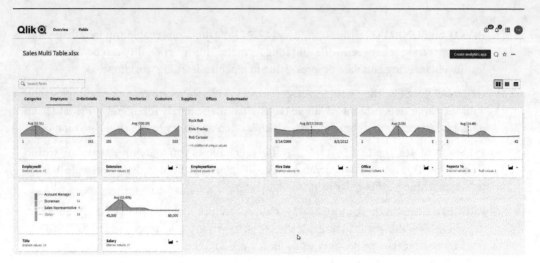

Figure 6.11: Data catalog

Here we can see a data distribution of all fields in the **Employees** entity. By default, we have **Tile view** open in our catalog. The following figure represents the tile of our **Salary** field. Let's take a closer look into that next:

Figure 6.12: The Salary field in the data catalog

The **Salary** tile will show us the minimum, average and maximum value of the **Salary** field. It will also tell us the number of distinct values. Using this information, we can already identify the possible outliers and get a preliminary understanding of the data distribution.

Next, we will change from **tile view** to **list view** using the small icon in the top-right corner (highlighted in the following figure). The following view should be visible:

Name	Data type	Distinct values	Null values	Sample values	
EmployeeID	INTEGER	47	0	1, 2, 3	
Extension	STRING	25	0	NULL, 500, 300	
EmployeeName	STRING	47	0	Rock Roll, Elvis Presley, Rob Carsson	
Hire Date	DATE	41	0	12/31/2011, 10/01/2009, 08/02/2010	
Office	INTEGER	5	0	3, 2, 4	
Reports To	INTEGER	16	1	4, 8, 22	
Title	STRING	10	0	Account Manager, Storeman, Sales Representative	
Salary	INTEGER	27	0	51,000, 50,000, 49,500	

Figure 6.13: Data catalog – list view

This view will tell us the data type of each field and the number of distinct and null values, and give a sample of values in each field. Data type and number of null values are especially valuable when starting to create a machine learning solution.

Next, we will continue our data validation using the data manager. We already covered some parts of the data manager in the previous section. We are using our `Sales Multi Table.xlsx` that was imported into the data manager, and we have opened our **Employees** entity for editing. Refer to the section covering the data manager earlier in this chapter if needed.

Next, we will activate the **EmployeeName** field. The data summary section should look like the following:

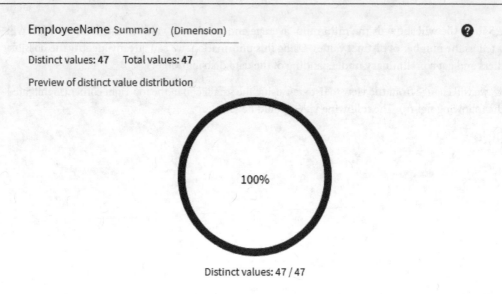

Figure 6.14: The EmployeeName field summary

Here we can see that this field is handled as a dimension, and we have 47 values in total. All the values are unique, and we can see the distribution. Next, we can activate the **Hire Date** field. The following summary is visible:

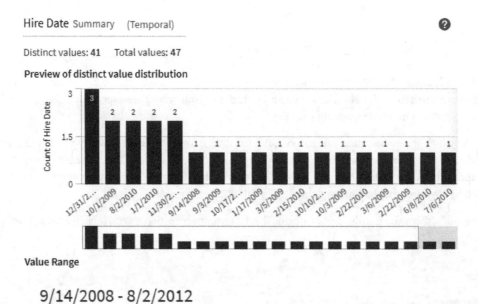

Figure 6.15: The Hire Date field summary

Here we can see the distribution of data and the number of total and distinct values. We can also see the value range for the data. This information is helpful when investigating the data and looking for potential outliers. Next, we can select the **Salary** field and we should see the following (you might need to change the type from dimension to measure):

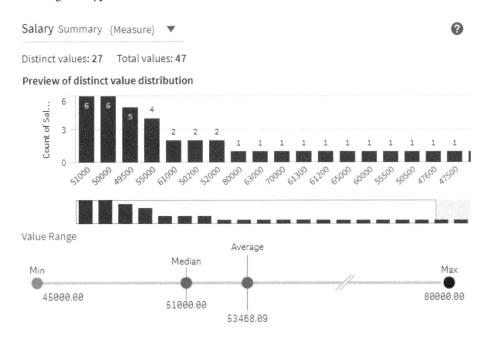

Figure 6.16: The Salary field summary

The **Salary** field summary will tell us the distribution, the number of total and distinct values, and the minimum, median, average, and maximum values. This information will help us further with our data investigation and validation.

The third option to validate data is to utilize Qlik's analytic objects and create a view on top of the data model. We will cover this in the later chapters of this book. Also, later in this chapter, we will look at Insight Advisor and how to use that to analyze data. Insight Advisor is a powerful tool for data validation.

Now that we have an overview of the data validation, we will investigate the possibilities of data lineage and data catalogs. These tools will help us to understand the data better and also help us to visualize the data pipelines.

Data lineage and data catalogs

In Qlik Sense, data lineage and data catalogs are two important features that help users to better understand, manage, and govern their data.

Data lineage refers to the path that data takes from its source to its destination, including all the transformations that occur along the way. In Qlik Sense, data lineage provides a visual representation of how data is transformed as it moves through the system. This helps users to understand the origin and quality of the data, as well as identify any issues or bottlenecks in the data flow. With data lineage, users can trace data back to its original source, identify any data dependencies, and ensure that the data is accurate and reliable.

A data catalog refers to a centralized repository of metadata that describes the data assets in an organization. In Qlik Sense, a data catalog provides a way to discover, understand, and collaborate on data assets. With a data catalog, users can search for data assets, view metadata and lineage information, and collaborate with others on the data. The data catalog also helps to ensure that data is properly governed, by providing a single source of truth for data definitions, data quality rules, and other important metadata.

Together, data lineage and data catalogs provide a comprehensive view of an organization's data assets, from its origin to its usage, enabling users to better understand and govern their data, and make informed decisions based on reliable information.

Let's take a closer look into both features next.

Data lineage

The data lineage feature can be found under the application options (the three dots on the right side of the application tile) in Qlik Cloud tenant. The following figure shows the **Lineage** option highlighted:

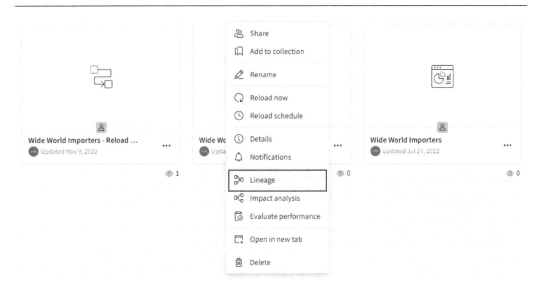

Figure 6.17: Qlik's Lineage function under application options

After selecting **Lineage**, a new view visualizing the whole lineage path for the selected application will open. An example of that view is visible in the following figure:

Figure 6.18: Data lineage view

The lineage view will show us how the data flows from the source systems into our end-user application. In this case our source system is an Azure SQL server, and we have a Qlik application called **QVD Generator** that will produce QVD files and store them in Qlik Cloud. These QVD files and files from other folders in our cloud environment are then used as base data for our end-user application, called **Wide World Importers**. It is also possible to view lineage at the table level. The following figure represents the lineage view for the **Countries** table found in our end-user application:

Figure 6.19: Data lineage for a single table in an end-user application

From this view we can easily verify what data is combined into the **Countries** table and where that data originated from.

Data lineage is a powerful tool for investigating the source and transformations of the data, and it is useful when working with data. It has a lot of features, and we only covered the most basic use case here. If you are interested in finding out more, there are a lot of materials available in Qlik Cloud's help pages.

Next, we will take a closer look at data catalogs and how to investigate individual data objects in more detail.

Data catalogs

We already discovered some of the data validation features of data catalogs in this chapter. Let's take a closer look at some of the other aspects of data catalogs next. We will start by opening the `Sales Multi Table.xlsx` file in Qlik Cloud. Once you have uploaded the file into the cloud, you should see the following tile:

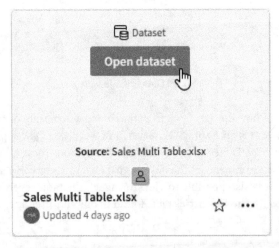

Figure 6.20: The Sales Multi Table.xlsx dataset tile

Select **Open dataset** and you will end up in the data catalog. Your view should look like the following:

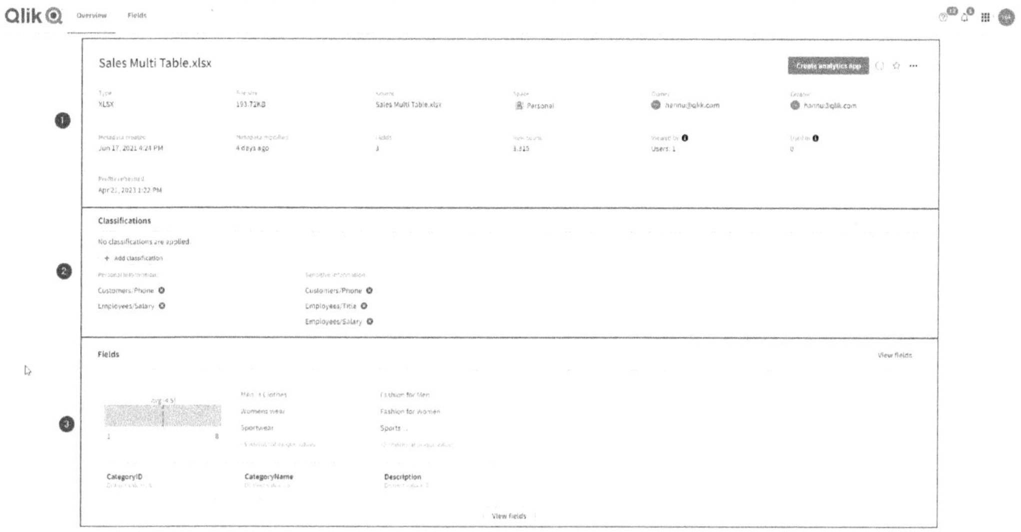

Figure 6.21: The data catalog's front page

The data catalog contains the following sections:

1. **Metadata**: This is general metadata about the file. This section will tell when the data is uploaded, where it is used, and who owns it. It will also give insights into the popularity of the dataset and the structure of the data.

2. **Classifications**: If any of the field is classified to personal information, sensitive or any other tag, this information can be seen here. If data is classified, we should be extremely careful when utilizing it. We can also set classifications on the dataset level using this section.

3. **Fields**: This section will give us an overview of the fields and the data in each field. This was already covered in more detail in the data validation section of this chapter.

Next, we can take a closer look at classifications. Let's move to the **Fields** tab and select the **Employees** entity. Under that we can select the **Salary** field. We should see the following:

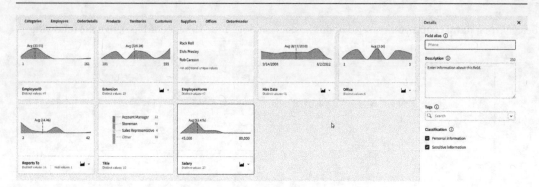

Figure 6.22: Data classification in the catalog

In the data classification view, we can give aliases to each field and provide them with a description. We can also tag individual fields and tell whether they contain personal or sensitive information. Augmenting information with tags and descriptions is important since many people in your organization might not be familiar with the data. Providing this information can also help us when creating a machine learning solution since we can get a better understanding of the data if additional information is provided.

The data catalog will help us to get familiar with the data and build a good collection of datasets. Next, we will take a closer look into Insight Advisor and how it can help us to get familiar with data and create visualizations easily.

Exploring data and finding insights

Qlik Insight Advisor is a feature in Qlik Sense that uses natural language processing and artificial intelligence to help users explore data and discover insights. By using Qlik Insight Advisor, you can leverage the power of natural language processing and AI to explore your data, ask questions, and discover meaningful insights.

In *Chapter 1*, we already learned some of the basics of Insight Advisor. It is also possible to explore data and find insights using Qlik objects and visualizations without the augmented intelligence features. We will take a closer look at how to create visualizations this way in a later section of this book. In this section, we will discover how Insight Advisor will help us to get meaningful insights out of the data.

We will begin by using the `Sales Multi Table.xlsx` file as our source data. We already created a data model on top of that dataset earlier in this chapter and loaded the data into an associative engine. After the data load is ready, we can select **Go to Sheet** and see the following three options:

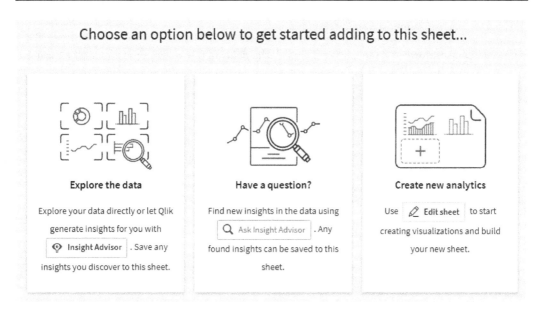

Figure 6.23: Options to discover data in the new application

In this case, we will select **Explore the data**. This will launch Insight Advisor and the following view should appear:

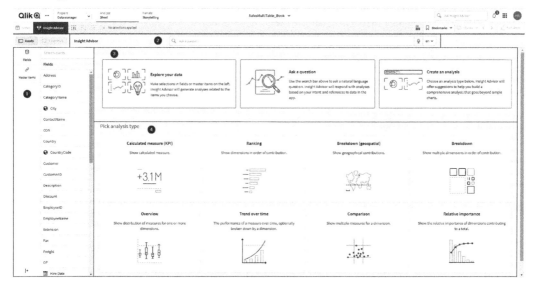

Figure 6.24: Insight Advisor

In this figure, we can see four different sections:

1. **Data exploration**: This segment contains all the fields in our source data and all the master items (if we have created these) in our applicatio.

2. **Natural language input**: This input field allows us to ask natural language questions from Insight Advisor

3. **Options**: This section will guide us to use different analysis types supported by Insight Advisor

4. **Analysis types**: This section will give us shortcuts to different analysis types

Let's start our data explorations by picking a field from a list in section one. We can select for example, the field called **Country**. The following view will appear giving us information about the data in the **Country** field:

Figure 6.25: Insight Advisor – field information

This view will show us the number of different countries as a KPI, a table showing all the countries by name, and a map showing the actual areas. We can return to the previous view by selecting **Cancel**.

Next, we will investigate guided analysis types. Let's start by selecting **Ranking** from the analysis type section. We should see the following:

Figure 6.26: Insight Advisor – ranking

In this view, we can select the measure and dimension to be used in our ranking graphs. Let's select **Sales** as a measure and **SalesOffice** as a dimension. This will give us our sales offices ranked by sales. We can see that Insight Advisor is using sum as an aggregator for the **Sales** field. This is correct in this case, but it can be modified if needed. Now we should see the following view:

Figure 6.27: Insight Advisor – ranking results

We can see that Insight Advisor generated a bar chart representing the total sales of each sales office for us. It also provided us with some additional information about the total sales and the best-performing sales offices. There are also alternative representations of the same data available.

We can add the bar chart to our sheet for further analysis, but it already tells us some important facts about the data. Next, we will investigate one of the more complex analyses. We can return to the previous view by selecting **Cancel** and select **Create an analysis**. The following screen showing all the available analysis types should appear:

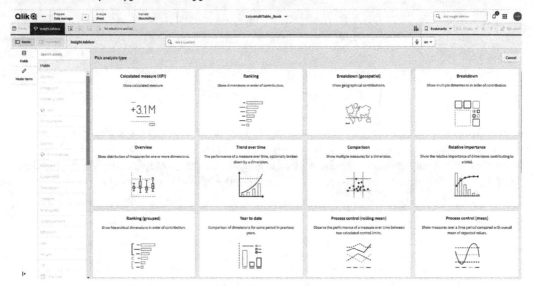

Figure 6.28: Insight Advisor – analysis types

From this list of analysis types, we will next investigate clustering. Select **Clustering (k-means)** from the list. Next, select the sum of **Sales** and the average of **Discount** as a measure and **ProductName** as a dimension. The following screen will appear:

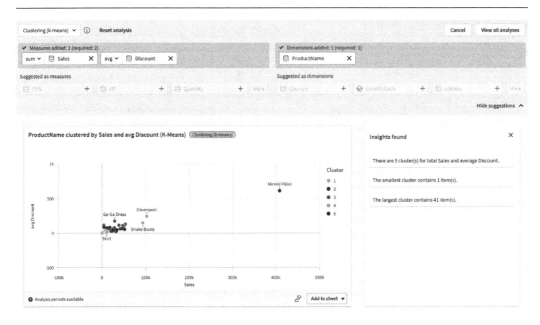

Figure 6.29: Insight Advisor – clustering

As we can see, there are five different groups of products recognized based on their total sales and average discounts. This will help us investigate our product sales more. We will also get additional information from Insight Advisor about the clusters. There are a lot of different analysis types supported and many are beneficial when exploring data for machine learning solutions. It is highly encouraged that you look at what all the analysis types do and what kind of results you can get.

Next, we will look at how the natural language input will work with Insight Advisor. We can first return to our base view by selecting **Cancel**. Now we can start typing an input into the field on top of the screen. Type the following query:

```
Give me total sales by CategoryName in each country
```

As we type our query, we can see that Insight Advisor will suggest different fields. The query will return the following view:

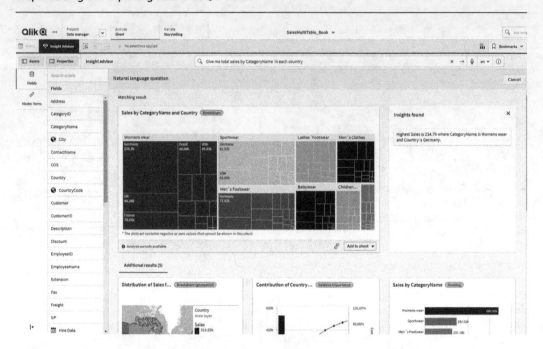

Figure 6.30: Insight Advisor – natural language query results

As we can see, Insight Advisor produced various graphs. We got a treemap representing the sales of each product category by country and map, a Pareto chart and a bar chart as alternative results. We also got some insights in written form.

Insight Advisor is a powerful tool to discover data and create visualizations. In this section, we touched on the basics of it. A lot more information can be found in Qlik's help pages. A good way to learn to use them is by playing around with some simple datasets.

Summary

In this chapter, we first got some hands-on experience with Qlik's data manager and learned how to create data models using it. We also learned how to create calculated fields and investigate data. Creating a good data model and modifying data to be suitable for machine learning is the key to success.

We also discovered some of the basics of Qlik scripting and how that can be used to perform data transformations. We discovered some of the important functions and features of Qlik script. Scripting is an alternative way to create a data model and manipulate data. It is a powerful tool and can be also combined with modeling created in the data manager.

In a later part of the chapter, we learned some methods of validating and investigating the data. We familiarized ourselves with the data catalog and data lineage views and learned to utilize them in data validation. Data validation is a key step in any machine learning or data analytics project, and it is important to understand the data before creating solutions on top of it.

The last part of this chapter taught us how to use Insight Advisor for data discovery. Insight Advisor is a powerful tool for conducting analysis using augmented intelligence and mastering it will help us get familiar with data faster.

In the next chapter, we will continue our hands-on journey and learn how to deploy and monitor machine learning models in both on-premises and cloud environments. This will create a good background for the last chapters of this book, where we will implement some more advanced models.

7

Deploying and Monitoring Machine Learning Models

In previous chapters, we learned a lot about different models and techniques. Understanding the concepts and building a machine learning model is only the beginning of the journey toward realizing its true value. The successful deployment and ongoing monitoring of these models are crucial to ensuring their effectiveness and reliability in real-world scenarios.

Ensuring that a model performs optimally, seamlessly integrates with existing systems, and adapts to evolving requirements requires a comprehensive understanding of the deployment process and the associated considerations. In the context of the Qlik platform, most of the typical pain points are handled by the platform itself and the design of the components, but there are still things we have to bear in mind.

Once a machine learning model is deployed, it is vital to continuously monitor its performance to identify potential issues, maintain accuracy, and safeguard against unforeseen failures. Monitoring provides insights into the model's behavior, helps detect data drift or concept drift, and facilitates the identification of performance degradation over time. By proactively monitoring and analyzing key metrics, organizations can make informed decisions regarding model maintenance, retraining, and updates as required to ensure reliable and up-to-date predictions.

In this chapter, we will get familiar with the following main topics:

- Building a model in an on-premises environment using Advanced Analytics Integration
- Monitoring and debugging models

This chapter focuses on on-premises environments. We will see how to deploy and monitor models using Qlik AutoML in our next chapter.

Building a model in an on-premises environment using the Advanced Analytics connection

In *Chapter 5*, we prepared an environment for R and Python using the Advanced Analytics connection with Qlik. In this chapter, we are going to utilize this same environment. This exercise will use R specifically.

In general, there are two ways to utilize the Advanced Analytics connection with Qlik applications. These are the following:

- **Live connection**: A live connection interacts with the third-party machine learning environment from the user interface while the user interacts with the application. A live connection enables *what-if* scenarios, simulations, and similar use cases. It is best for light models that do not require extensive training. The idea behind live connections is explained in the following diagram:

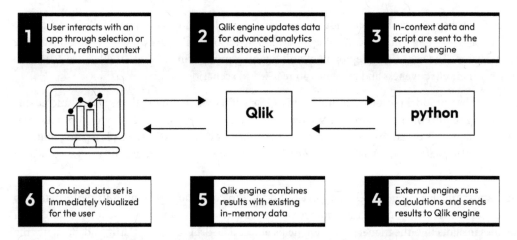

Figure 7.1: Advanced Analytics connection

- **Load time connection**: A load time connection is a one-time prediction model run that takes place when a Qlik load script is executed. When the Advanced Analytics connection is utilized during load time, the results are saved into a table in the Qlik data model. These results can be then utilized when creating an application. A load time connection is suitable for use cases that only require one predicted value. For example, if we are predicting the future value of the sales of a product and would like to save the prediction in the data model for later analysis, a load time connection is used. It is also good for models that require extensive training. It is possible to combine a live connection with a load time connection to predict some values when data is loaded and utilize scenario analysis interactively.

> **Note**
>
> A prepared model can be saved and reused during load time or in live mode. This way we can save some time during deployment if the parameters of a model haven't changed and it is known to have performed well previously. To save a model in R, for example, we can use the following commands:
>
> Using the `saveRDS()` and `readRDS()` functions: This method allows you to save any R object, including machine learning models, to a file using the `saveRDS()` function and reload it using `readRDS()`.
>
> Using the `save()` and `load()` functions: The `save()` function allows you to save multiple R objects, including models, to a file in binary format, which can be loaded using the `load()` function.
>
> Using specific package functions: Some machine learning packages in R provide their own dedicated functions for saving and loading models. For example, if you're using the `caret` package, you can use the `saveModel()` and `loadModel()` functions.

In the next hands-on example, we will utilize the Advanced Analytics connection during load time and create a simple K-means clustering model. To begin with, we should have our R environment running and our `Sales Multi Table.xlsx` loaded in the Qlik application with the prepared data model.

In the following example, we would like to create clusters based on product categories, sales, and average discounts to examine how different product categories will produce sales compared to given discounts. We will also create a slicer to control the number of clusters presented.

We will begin by creating a simple layout for our application. We will add a scatter plot object, a bar chart, a filter pane, a slicer for variables, and two KPI objects to the sheet. It should look like the following screenshot:

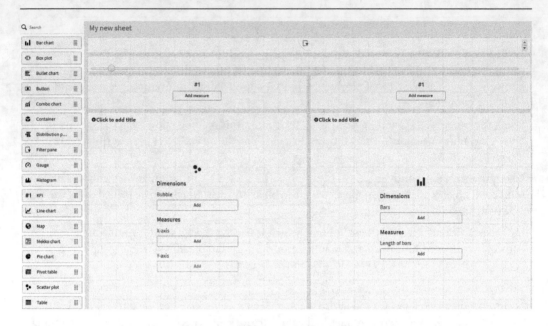

Figure 7.2: Layout for clustering example

To add a slicer for variable input, the dashboard extension bundle needs to be installed. Create a variable named `clusters` and set its default value to 4. The settings for the variable and variable input are presented respectively in the following screenshots:

Figure 7.3: Variable settings

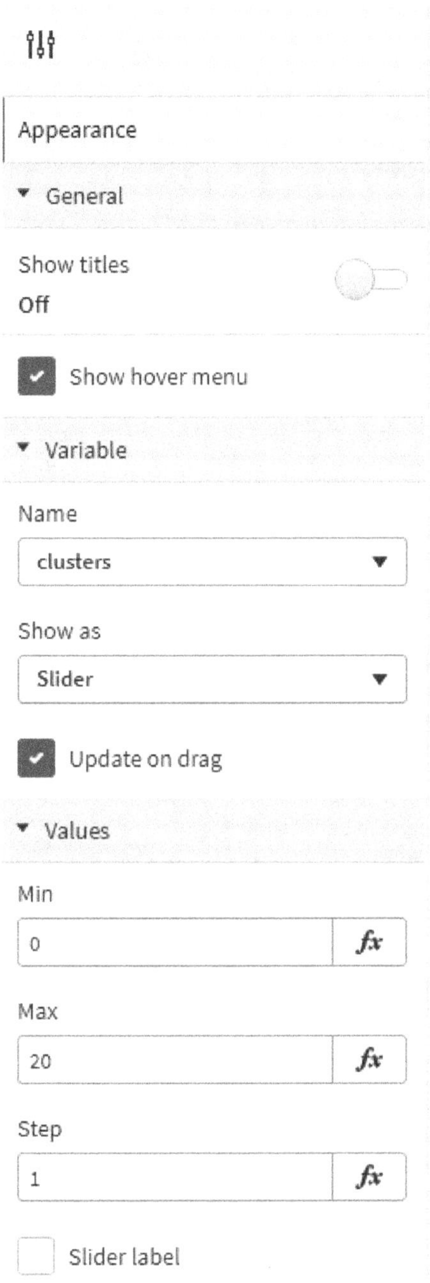

Figure 7.4: Variable input settings

Next, we configure our scatter plot and start creating our cluster model. Begin by adding `ProductName` as a dimension, `sum(Sales)` as the *x*-axis measure, and `avg(Discount)` as the *y*-axis measure. This should produce the following graph:

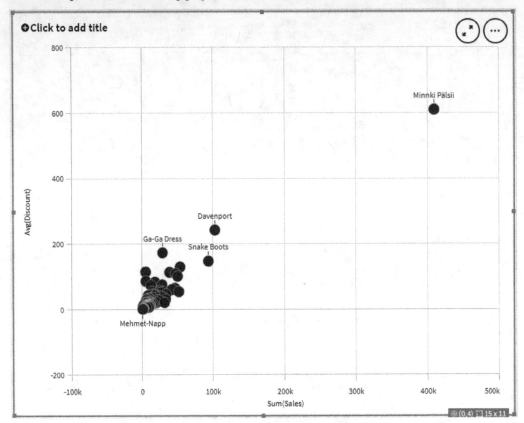

Figure 7.5: Scatter plot with dimensions and measures

We would like the bubble color to be defined using the cluster model from R. Let's start by selecting **Appearance → Colors and legend**. Turn off the auto coloring and select **Color by expression**.

Enter the following formula in the **Expression** field:

```
R.ScriptEval('
q$id <- 1:nrow(q);
F2 <- q[order(q$sales,q$discount),];
F3 <- data.frame(sales=F2$sales ,discount=F2$discount);
rows <- nrow(F2);
if(rows >= $(clusters)){
    set.seed(5);
    clusterdata <- kmeans(F3,$(clusters),nstart = 20);
```

```
    df <- data.frame(rowid=F2$id,data=clusterdata$cluster);
     out <- df[order(df$rowid),];
}else{
     out$data <- c(rep(1,rows))
}
out$data',
Sum(Sales) as sales,
avg(Discount) as discount)
```

The preceding code starts with the R.ScriptEval function, which tells the Qlik engine that the expression should be executed using the Advanced Analytics connection. R is the connection name and ScriptEval is the function used in this example. In total, the following expression types are supported by the R **server-side extension (SSE)**:

Function Name	Function Type	Argument Type	Return Type
ScriptEval	Scalar, Tensor	Numeric	Numeric
ScriptEvalStr	Scalar, Tensor	String	String
ScriptAggr	Aggregation	Numeric	Numeric
ScriptAggrStr	Aggregation	String	String
ScriptEvalEx	Scalar, Tensor	Numeric or String	Numeric
ScriptEvalExStr	Scalar, Tensor	Numeric or String	String
ScriptAggrEx	Aggregation	Numeric or String	Numeric
ScriptAggrExStr	Aggregation	Numeric or String	String
ScriptEvalEx	Scalar, Tensor	Numeric or String	Numeric

Table 7.1: Functions supported by the R SSE

After the initial function call, we can write our actual R code. In the preceding example, we use the k-means function to calculate the cluster number for each of our products. The last two lines are data taken from Qlik and passed to the R environment. The Qlik engine creates a dataframe named q that contains the data sent. In this case, it contains our aggregated sales as q$sales and our discount as q$discount. We are using our previously created variable clusters to describe the number of clusters in our code. The following is a step-by-step breakdown of the code:

1. q$id <- 1:nrow(q): This line creates a new column in the q dataframe called id and assigns it values from 1 to the number of rows in 0071. This column is used to preserve the original row order during sorting and clustering.

2. F2 <- q[order(q$sales, q$discount),]: Here, the q dataframe is sorted in ascending order based on the sales column first, and then within each sales value, it is sorted based on the discount column. The sorted data is stored in the F2 dataframe.

3. `F3 <- data.frame(sales = F2$sales, discount = F2$discount)`: This line creates a new `F3` dataframe that contains only the `sales` and `discount` columns from `F2`. It essentially extracts those two columns for further processing.

4. `rows <- nrow(F2)`: This line calculates the number of rows in the `F2` dataframe and assigns it to the `rows` variable.

5. `if(rows >= clusters) { ... } else { ... }`: This is an if-else statement that checks whether the number of rows in `F2` is greater than or equal to the value of the `clusters` variable. If it is, clustering is performed; otherwise, a default value of `1` is assigned to all rows.

6. `set.seed(5)`: This line sets a seed value for reproducible results in the clustering algorithm. The seed value of `5` is used in this case.

7. `clusterdata <- kmeans(F3, clusters, nstart = 20)`: This line applies the k-means clustering algorithm to the `F3` dataframe. The `clusters` variable determines the number of clusters to be formed, and `nstart = 20` specifies the number of times the algorithm will be restarted with different initial cluster assignments.

8. `df <- data.frame(rowid = F2$id, data = clusterdata$cluster)`: Here, a new `df` dataframe is created with two columns, `rowid` and `data`. The `rowid` column contains the original row identifiers from `F2`, and the `data` column contains the cluster assignments obtained from the `clusterdata` object.

9. `out <- df[order(df$rowid), ]`: This line rearranges the rows of the `df` dataframe in the original row order by sorting based on the `rowid` column. The sorted dataframe is stored in the `out` variable.

10. `out$data`: Finally, this line retrieves the `data` column from the `out` dataframe, which represents the cluster assignments or the default value of `1` for each row.

Qlik takes the data field from the `out` dataframe and assigns values to each product name. We can then use the cluster number as our color dimension in our scatter plot.

To get visible results, we should disable the **The expression is a color code** setting and select **Diverging classes** as the color scheme. The result with five clusters (you can use the slicer to set the variable value to five) should look like the following screenshot:

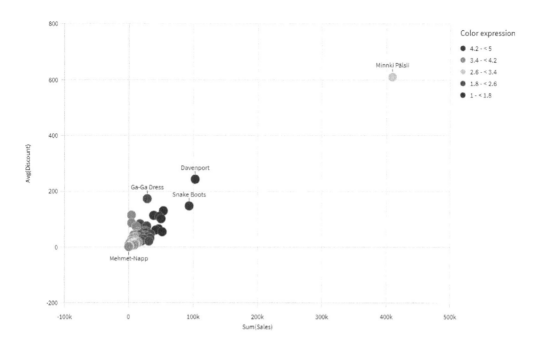

Figure 7.6: Scatterplot with clusters as color

As you can see, we have five different groups of items that have similar characteristics in terms of total sales and the average discount applied. The cluster number can be seen if you hover over the single bubble.

> **Note**
>
> Using master items is always encouraged. In production environments, clusters should be created as master items. This way, changes made to the model will be inherited by all graphs.

As a final step, we can finish our layout. Insert **sum(Sales)** and **avg(Discount)** into KPI objects and take some dimensions into filter pane. Finally, add sales by product name into bar chart. You should get a view that looks like the following:

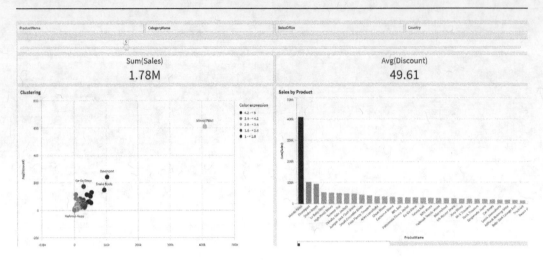

Figure 7.7: Final layout

We have now successfully created our first model using R and Advanced Analytics Integration. Next, we will take a closer look at debugging and monitoring. We will implement another model with a slightly more advanced use case in *Chapter 10*.

Monitoring and debugging models

Debugging a model during development is a crucial development step. With Advanced Analytics Integration in on-premises environments, we have several options to debug our model and figure out how it is performing.

The first and most logical place to start debugging in an interactive scenario is to look at the chart output. If there is something wrong with the code, you will get an error message here. In the following example, we can see that a library called `forecast` is missing from the environment:

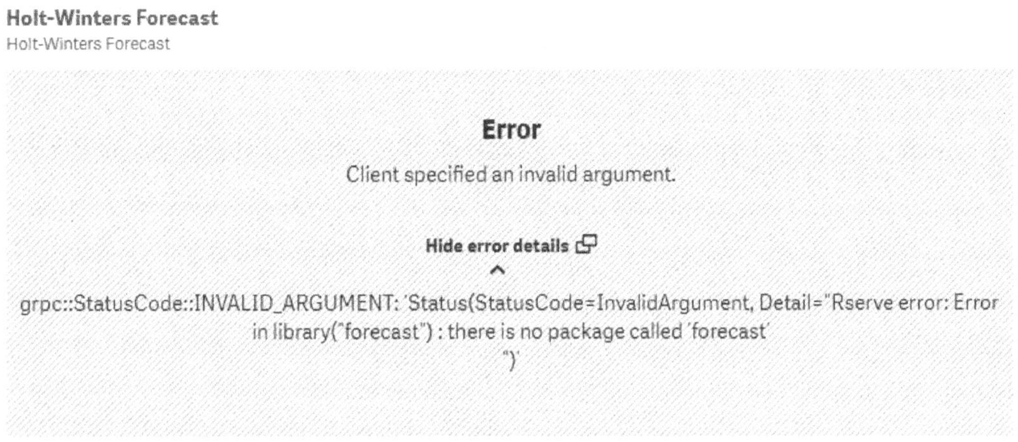

Holt-Winters Forecast
Holt-Winters Forecast

Error

Client specified an invalid argument.

Hide error details

^

grpc::StatusCode::INVALID_ARGUMENT: 'Status(StatusCode=InvalidArgument, Detail="Rserve error: Error in library("forecast") : there is no package called 'forecast'
")'

Figure 7.8: Error message in chart

Sometimes, you may need more comprehensive information or debug prints from the actual R code. Since R is running as a service, there is no easy way to get debug prints during execution. You can, however, use file writing. Returning to our previous Rserve example, adding the following code will produce a file called debug.txt in our Rserve home folder (the added code is shown in **bold**):

```
R.ScriptEval('
q$id <- 1:nrow(q);
F2 <- q[order(q$sales,q$discount),];
F3 <- data.frame(sales=F2$sales ,discount=F2$discount);
rows <- nrow(F2);

write(c("----------------"),file="debug.txt",append=TRUE);
summary<-summary(q);
head<-capture.output(head(q))
write(summary,file="debug.txt",append=TRUE);
write(c("----------------"),file="debug.txt",append=TRUE);
write(head,file="debug.txt",append=TRUE);
write(c("----------------"),file="debug.txt",append=TRUE);

if(rows >= $(clusters)){
    set.seed(5);
    clusterdata <- kmeans(F3,$(clusters),nstart = 20);
   df <- data.frame(rowid=F2$id,data=clusterdata$cluster);
    out <- df[order(df$rowid),];
}else{
    out$data <- c(rep(1,rows))
}
```

```
out$data',
Sum(Sales) as sales,
avg(Discount) as discount)
```

The preceding code will print a summary of the q dataframe and a sample of it using the `capture.output` function. The result file will look like the following:

```
----------------
Min.    :    348.8
1st Qu.:   6491.4
Median :  10984.5
Mean    :  23157.8
3rd Qu.:  25525.6
Max.    : 408674.5
Min.    :    1.224
1st Qu.:   11.709
Median :   28.048
Mean    :   47.583
3rd Qu.:   52.524
Max.    :  609.970
Min.    : 1
1st Qu.:20
Median :39
Mean    :39
3rd Qu.:58
Max.    :77
----------------
       sales discount id
1   6833.144 15.36303  1
2   7815.963 11.11661  2
3  13523.793 15.85746  3
4  24966.158 41.04122  4
5   3633.208 11.70914  5
6  15295.435 45.96056  6
----------------
```

> **Note**
> You can define the file path in the file parameter if so desired. If a path is not defined, the file will be written to the `Rserve` home directory. An example path is `C:\Program Files\R\R-4.3.0\library\Rserve\libs\x64`.

If you need to debug the operation of the bridge component, there are log files stored in the /logs folder under the root directory of the server-side extension. Log files are created and stored daily. If there is something wrong with the code execution, these log files are a good way to start debugging. You can also monitor the returned data and execution times using these log files. The following is some sample input written during the execution of our clustering example:

```
2023-05-30 21:12:10.3865 INFO EvaluateScript called from client
(ipv6:[::1]:49924), hashid (38116153)
2023-05-30 21:12:10.3865 DEBUG EvaluateScript header info: AppId
(bedcb600-18c3-4e6e-a1dc-55562ac21e48), UserId (UserDirectory=QMI-QS-
06C0; UserId=qmi), Cardinality (77 rows)
2023-05-30 21:12:10.3865 INFO EvaluateScript call with
hashid(38116153) got Param names:  sales discount
2023-05-30 21:12:10.3865 DEBUG Evaluating R script, hashid (38116153):
q$id <- 1:nrow(q);
F2 <- q[order(q$sales,q$discount),];
F3 <- data.frame(sales=F2$sales ,discount=F2$discount);
rows <- nrow(F2);

write(c("----------------"),file="debug.txt",append=TRUE);
summary<-summary(q);
head<-capture.output(head(q))
write(summary,file="debug.txt",append=TRUE);
write(c("----------------"),file="debug.txt",append=TRUE);
write(head,file="debug.txt",append=TRUE);
write(c("----------------"),file="debug.txt",append=TRUE);

if(rows >= 4){
    set.seed(5);
    clusterdata <- kmeans(F3,4,nstart = 20);
    df <- data.frame(rowid=F2$id,data=clusterdata$cluster);
    out <- df[order(df$rowid),];
}else{
    out$data <- c(rep(1,rows))
}
out$data
2023-05-30 21:12:10.4115 INFO Rserve result: 77 rows, hashid
(38116153)
2023-05-30 21:12:10.4115 DEBUG Took 23 ms, hashid (38116153)
```

The preceding log entry first gives us some information about incoming requests from the Qlik engine. It details which user is making the call and from what application. It also tells us the cardinality of the data. This information is important when evaluating performance.

Next, we get information about the function used and the parameters passed from Qlik. It will also print the entire code into the log if DEBUG-level is enabled. Finally, we get information about the total execution time and the rows returned. These log entries are a good starting point when evaluating model performance. More comprehensive performance metrics can be written into the model code and evaluated using the method described previously in this section.

Summary

In this chapter, we took a closer look at model creation and deployment using Advanced Analytics Integration and the server-side R extension in an on-premises environment (having done the initial environment setup in *Chapter 5*).

We started our journey in this chapter by getting familiar with the two concepts of utilizing Advanced Analytics Integration. We then took a closer look at an on-the-fly data analytics use case and created a k-means clustering example with real-time integration with R.

We built a simple dashboard to support our analysis and took a deeper look at the Advanced Analytics Integration syntax. In the latter part of this chapter, we learned how to debug and monitor our models running in on-premises environments.

In the next chapter, we will shift our focus toward Qlik AutoML. We will learn the implementation model used with AutoML and how to utilize this tool both in Qlik Cloud and on-premises. We will also learn how to deploy and monitor models using AutoML.

8

Utilizing Qlik AutoML

Qlik AutoML leverages the power of artificial intelligence and automation to empower users of all skill levels to build and deploy machine learning models, without the need for extensive coding or data science backgrounds. By automating repetitive tasks and providing intelligent recommendations, Qlik AutoML streamlines the entire machine learning workflow, making it accessible to a broader audience.

In this chapter, we will delve into the world of Qlik AutoML, exploring its capabilities, benefits, and practical applications. We will provide a comprehensive overview of the underlying concepts and techniques that enable Qlik AutoML to automate the machine learning process. Moreover, we will guide you through the step-by-step implementation of AutoML models within the Qlik ecosystem, highlighting its seamless integration with the Qlik Sense analytics platform.

In this chapter, we will cover the following topics:

- Features of Qlik AutoML
- Using Qlik AutoML in a cloud environment
- Creating and monitoring a machine learning model with Qlik AutoML
- Connecting Qlik AutoML to an on-premises environment
- Best practices with Qlik AutoML

Features of Qlik AutoML

Qlik AutoML is a tool within the Qlik Sense analytics platform that automates the process of building and deploying machine learning models. It simplifies the machine learning workflow and allows users to create predictive models, without requiring in-depth knowledge of data science or programming. Some of the key features of Qlik AutoML include the following:

- **Automated model selection**: Qlik AutoML automatically selects the best machine learning algorithm based on data and the prediction task, saving users from manually exploring and comparing different algorithms.

- **Hyperparameter tuning**: Qlik AutoML optimizes the hyperparameters of the selected machine learning model to improve its performance and accuracy. Hyperparameter tuning helps fine-tune the model's behavior and makes it more effective in making predictions.

- **Cross-validation**: Qlik AutoML uses cross-validation techniques to evaluate the performance of models. It splits data into multiple subsets and trains and tests the models on different combinations, providing more robust performance metrics.

- **Model evaluation**: Qlik AutoML provides various performance metrics to evaluate models, such as accuracy, precision, recall, and the F1 score. These metrics help users assess the model's predictive power and choose the best-performing model for their use case.

- **Model deployment**: Once the model is built and selected, Qlik AutoML enables easy deployment within the Qlik Sense environment. Users can seamlessly integrate the predictive models into their existing Qlik apps and dashboards for real-time insights and decision-making.

> **Note**
>
> Some of the features (including hyperparameter optimization and the prediction API) will require a paid tier of Qlik AutoML. Also, the number of deployments, concurrent tasks, and dataset limits are defined by license tier. Specific tier limits should be verified by Qlik Sales.

Qlik AutoML aims to democratize machine learning and empower business users to leverage advanced analytics capabilities, without extensive technical expertise. In *Chapter 4*, we looked at the general concepts in creating a good machine learning solution.

As you might remember from that chapter, there are three types of machine learning problems that Qlik AutoML can solve:

- **Binary classification**: Any question that can be answered with a yes or no

- **Multi-class classification**: Questions where there could be multiple outcome choices

- **Regression/numeric**: Predicting a number at a future point

Qlik AutoML is available as part of the Qlik Cloud offering. In the following section, we will get familiar with the actual process of getting a deployed, production-ready model from our training data.

Using Qlik AutoML in a cloud environment

There are several steps when deploying a machine learning model using Qlik AutoML. These steps are illustrated in the following diagram:

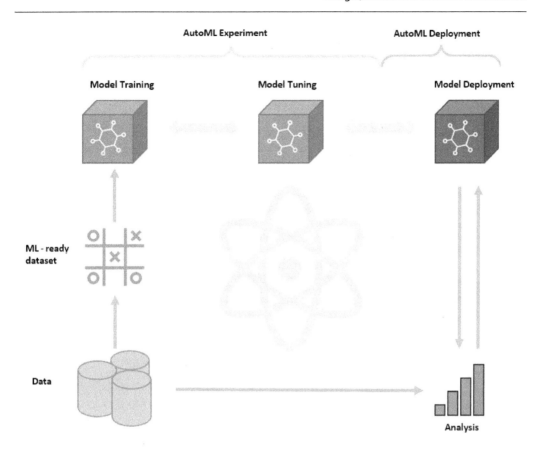

Figure 8.1: The AutoML workflow

As you might remember from our earlier chapters, the first step of every machine learning project is to define a business problem and question, followed by the steps required for data cleaning, preparation, and modeling. Typically, data cleaning and transformation part can take up 80–90% of the time spent on a project.

Once we have a machine-learning-ready dataset, we will continue by creating a machine learning experiment.

In automated machine learning, the process of training machine learning algorithms on a specific dataset and target is automated. When you create an experiment and load your dataset, the system automatically examines and prepares data for machine learning. It provides you with statistics and insights about each column, aiding in the selection of a target variable. Once the training begins, multiple algorithms analyze the data, searching for patterns.

Upon completion of the training process, you can assess the performance of the generated machine learning models using scores and rankings. By adjusting parameters and repeating the training, you can generate multiple versions of the models. After carefully evaluating the options, you can choose the model that performs best on your dataset. An experiment can have multiple versions, each using one or more algorithms, and one experiment can result in several machine learning deployments.

Simply, during the experiment phase, we will fine-tune the model and try to achieve the best possible accuracy. Once we are happy with the model, we can deploy it into production and start utilizing it in our analysis. We will go through each of these steps in our hands-on example in the following section.

Creating and monitoring a machine learning model with Qlik AutoML

In this section, we will create an actual implementation using Qlik AutoML. We will utilize the famous Iris dataset that we have already used in this book. The data preparation part for Iris dataset is already done, so we can jump into the model training and experiment part directly.

> **Note**
> You can find the datasets used in this example in the GitHub repository for this book.

> **Note**
> Only users with Professional entitlement can create experiments. This is a limitation at the license level.

Let's assume that we have already uploaded the `iris` dataset into our cloud tenant. Now, we will start to define a business question. This question defines what we would like to achieve from our machine learning model.

As we know, the Iris dataset consists of measurements of four features of three different species of Iris flowers. These features are as follows:

- **Sepal length**: The length of the sepal, which is the outermost part of the flower that protects the petals
- **Sepal width**: The width of the sepal
- **Petal length**: The length of the petals, which are the colorful leaf-like structures inside the flower
- **Petal width**: The width of the petals

The dataset contains 150 instances or samples, with 50 samples for each of the three Iris species – `setosa`, `versicolor`, and `virginica`. To define a machine learning question to predict species in the Iris dataset, we will frame it as a multi-class classification problem. Here is a sample question that we will form before our investigation:

Given the measurements of sepal length, sepal width, petal length, and petal width, can we accurately classify the species of Iris flowers into setosa, versicolor, or virginica?

In this case, the machine learning task involves training a model to learn the patterns and relationships between the input features (sepal length, sepal width, petal length, and petal width) and the corresponding output classes (`setosa`, `versicolor`, and `virginica`). The goal is to develop a predictive model that can accurately classify new instances of iris flowers into one of the three species, based on their measurements. AutoML will choose the best-performing model for us, based on the selected target and variables.

We will begin the actual model creation by creating a new machine learning experiment. To do that, select + **Add new** → **New ML experiment**, as shown in the following screenshot:

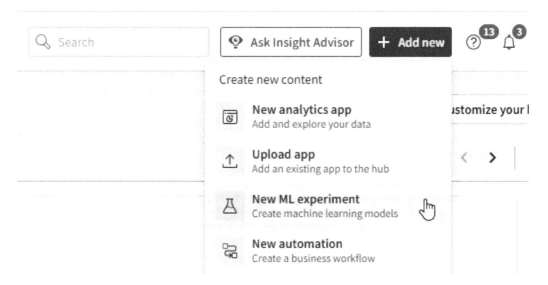

Figure 8.2: A new machine learning experiment

A new window will open. Insert a name for your new experiment, and select a space for it. In my example, I will call the experiment `Iris exp`. Select **Create** to proceed.

Then, you can select a dataset for training. Select `iris.csv`, which we uploaded earlier to our tenant. A preview window will open. In this window, we will define our target field. It will also give us important information about the dataset. You should see a preview window like the following:

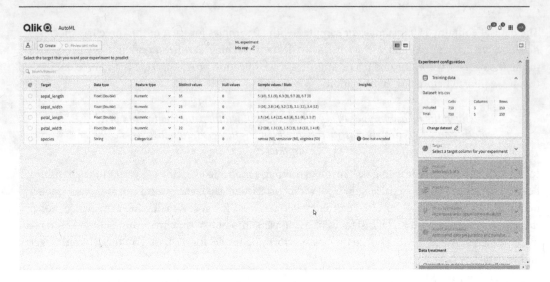

Figure 8.3: Schema view in the machine learning experiment wizard

You are currently in **schema view**. In this view, you can see the features (columns) in our dataset as a list. You will also see the data types that AutoML has recognized – for example, `String` for the `species` field and `Float (Double)` for other fields.

All columns have been recognized as `Numeric` or `Categorical` fields. This can be changed for each field if needed. We can also see from the `Insights` column that our "species" feature has been automatically one-hot encoded. If there are any warnings related to some of the features, we can also see these. The following information is presented in the `Insights` column:

- **Constant**: The column has the same value for all rows. The column can't be used as a target or included feature. This is a pre-set limitation in Qlik AutoML to prevent incorrect results.

- **One-hot encoded**: The feature type is categorical, and the column has fewer than 14 unique values.

- **Impact encoded**: The feature type is categorical, and the column has 14 or more unique values.

- **High cardinality**: The column has too many unique values and can negatively affect model performance if used as a feature. The column can't be used as a target.

- **Sparse data**: The column has too many `null` values. The column can't be used as a target or included feature.

- **Underrepresented class**: The column has a class with fewer than 10 rows. Column can't be used as a target but can be included as a feature.

Before selecting our target field, we can change our view to **data view**. You can do this from the top-right corner of the data preview area. You should see the following view:

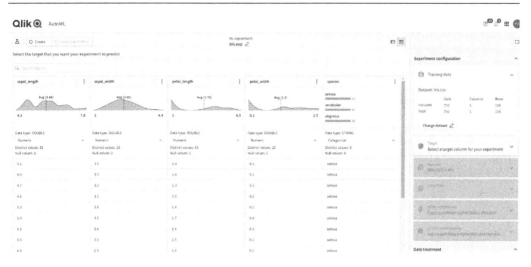

Figure 8.4: Data view in the machine learning experiment wizard

In this view, we can investigate the data content more. We will see a mini-chart representing the distribution of data in each numerical field, as well as the distribution in categorical fields. We will also get information about the distinct and `null` values.

Let's now change back to schema view and select our `species` feature as a target. To do this, select `species`, as shown in the following screenshot:

	Target	Data type	Feature type		Distinct values	Null values	Sample values / Stats	Insights
	sepal_length	Float (Double)	Numeric	⌄	35	0	5 (10), 5.1 (9), 6.3 (9), 5.7 (8), 6.7 (8)	
	sepal_width	Float (Double)	Numeric	⌄	23	0	3 (26), 2.8 (14), 3.2 (13), 3.1 (12), 3.4 (12)	
	petal_length	Float (Double)	Numeric	⌄	43	0	1.5 (14), 1.4 (12), 4.5 (8), 5.1 (8), 1.3 (7)	
	petal_width	Float (Double)	Numeric	⌄	22	0	0.2 (28), 1.3 (13), 1.5 (12), 1.8 (12), 1.4 (8)	
	Select as target	String	Categorical	⌄	3	0	setosa (50), versicolor (50), virginica (50)	ⓘ One-hot encoded

Figure 8.5: Target selection

All the other features are automatically included in our experiment. In this case, we want to keep all features included, but typically, we might want to drop some of the fields. On the right side, we can see the summary information about the experiment:

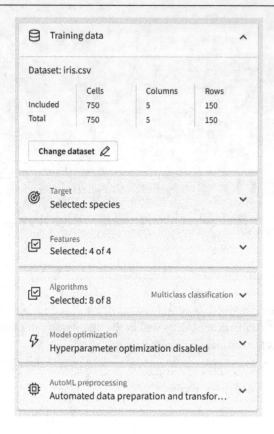

Figure 8.6: The experiment summary

First, we get a summary of our training data. We will see the total amount of cells, columns, and rows in a dataset and how many of those have been included in the experiment. In our case, all data is included, since we decided to keep all the features in our experiment.

Now, we can see some information about our target. We can also change the target before running our experiment. In this case, our target is species. The following section will give us a summary of the selected features. We will select all the features from our data as part of our experiment.

In the algorithm section, we can see that AutoML has identified our model to be a multiclass classification, based on our target field. We can decide to exclude some algorithms from our experiment if we want. Typically, it is recommended to keep all algorithms included.

Under model optimization, we can enable hyperparameter optimization and set the maximum time for our experiment to run optimization. Hyperparameter optimization will create a series of models from a methodical search for the optimal combination of algorithm hyperparameters, maximizing model performance. An experiment can take a long time to run if this option is enabled, but results can be more accurate.

Ultimately, we will get a reminder of the preprocessing steps that AutoML will take care of for us. These are as follows:

1. **Imputation of nulls**: AutoML automatically fills in missing and `null` values in features that have at least 50% of the values populated. Depending on each feature's data type, AutoML selects MEAN or OTHER imputation.

2. **Encoding categorical features**: AutoML automatically converts your categorical features to numerical values so that algorithms can effectively process and learn from your categorical training data. For features with 13 or fewer values, AutoML uses one-hot encoding. For features with 14 or more values, AutoML uses impact encoding.

3. **Feature scaling**: AutoML uses feature scaling to normalize the range of independent variables in your training data. AutoML calculates the mean and standard deviation for each column, and then it calculates the number of standard deviations away from the mean for each row.

4. **Automatic holdout of training data**: AutoML extracts 20% of your training dataset to be used for final model evaluation. AutoML *holds* that data until after model training, when it is used to evaluate the performance of the model. The benefit of holdout data is that it is not seen by the model during training (unlike cross-validation data), so it is ideal to validate model performance.

5. **Five-fold cross-validation**: After applying the previous preprocessing steps, AutoML randomly sorts your remaining training data into five distinct groups called "folds" for use in cross-validation. AutoML tests each fold against a model trained using the other four folds. In other words, each trained model is tested on a piece of data that the model has never seen before.

We are now ready with our experiment setup and can proceed by selecting **Run experiment**. The actual model preprocessing and training phase will start; it will take a while to finish. After the experiment has finished running the models, we will see the **Model metrics** screen, as shown in the following screenshot:

Figure 8.7: Model metrics

We can see that the top-performing model was the XGBoost Classification algorithm, with an `F1 Macro` score of `0.967`. We also get information about the `F1 Micro`, `F1 Weighted`, and `Accuracy` scores. We covered the meaning of the F1 score in the first chapter. The difference between the micro, macro, and weighted F1 scores is the following:

- Macro F1 is the averaged F1 value for each class without weighting (all classes are treated equally).

- Micro F1 is the F1 value calculated across the entire confusion matrix. Calculating the micro F1 score is equivalent to calculating the global precision or global recall.

- Weighted F1 corresponds to the binary classification F1. It is calculated for each class and then combined as a weighted average, considering the number of records for each class.

As you might remember, accuracy measures how often a model makes a correct prediction on average. In our case, the accuracy score is 0.967, meaning that our model is correct ~97% of cases.

Under `Hyperparameters`, we can also investigate the model parameters. For our top-performing model, these look like the following:

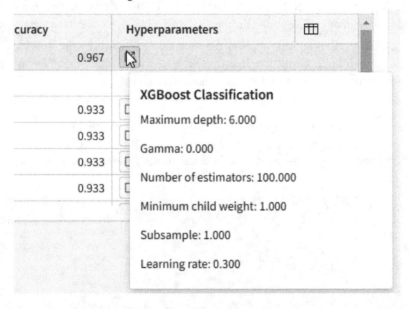

Figure 8.8: Hyperparameters for XGBoost classification

These are meant to give us more detailed information about the model. Parameters are algorithm-specific.

Now, we will take a closer look at the **Permutation importance** and **SHAP importance** diagrams. We explored the basic concept of both diagrams in *Chapter 1*. The following figure shows an example of the diagrams:

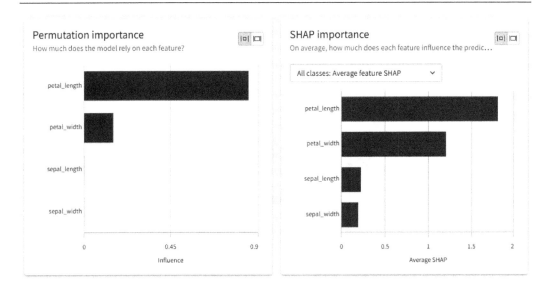

Figure 8.9: The Permutation importance and SHAP importance diagrams

As you might remember, permutation importance is a measure of how important a feature is to the overall prediction of a model. Basically, it describes how the model would be affected if you removed its ability to learn from that feature. AutoML uses the scikit-learn toolkit to calculate permutation importance.

SHAP importance is a method used to interpret the predictions of machine learning models. It provides insights into the contribution of each feature to the prediction for a specific instance, or a group of instances. Basically, it represents how a feature influences the prediction of a single row, relative to the other features in that row and to the average outcome in the dataset. SHAP importance is measured at the row level, and AutoML uses various algorithms to calculate the SHAP importance score.

From the preceding graphs, we can see that **petal_length** is an important feature in our prediction, both in terms of permutation and SHAP importance. In multiclass problems, we can also investigate the SHAP importance for each class. Let's investigate our SHAP values for each feature by class. Change a graph type using the drop-down menu on the SHAP chart, and select **Feature SHAP by class**. You should see the following graph:

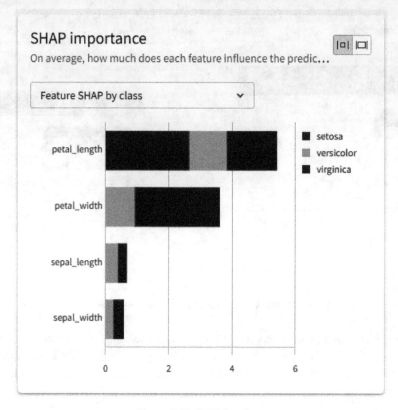

Figure 8.10: SHAP by class

From the preceding graph, we can see that **petal_length** can be used to distinguish **setosa** from **versicolor** and **virginica**. Other features are then used to determine the species further. We can also see the SHAP importance for each specific class if we change the graph type from the drop-down menu.

If we want to change our experiment, we can select **Configure v2** and modify the parameters for it. In this case, we are happy with our model. To deploy our model, we can select **Deploy**. We can provide a name for our model if we are not happy with the autogenerated one and decide a space for it. AutoML autofills some details about the model in the **Description** field. Make sure that the **Enable real-time API access** option is enabled, and select **Deploy**. Then, select **Open** from the popup, and you should get redirected to our new machine learning model. You should then see a view like the following:

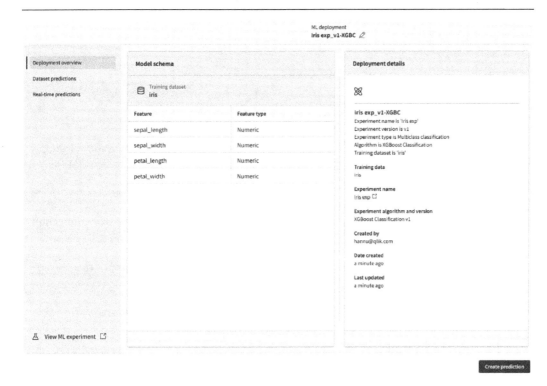

Figure 8.11: The deployed machine learning model

On the left-hand side, you can see a schema for the deployed model. The schema will tell us what kind of data our model expects when using it for predictions. On the right side, we can see details about our model. The other two tabs will give us information about predictions that were run manually and the REST endpoint connectivity. Take a closer look at these, and return to schema view when you are done.

We can use our model directly by selecting **Create prediction** and uploading a CSV or other data file for our model. This way, we will get our results stored as a file in Qlik Cloud. There is also a possibility to schedule predictions and apply dynamic naming for result files. However, a more robust way to utilize our new model is to use it through a data connector. Let's take a closer look into that next.

For our application, we will use another dataset called `iris_test.csv`. To begin, upload the file to Qlik Cloud. Create a new Qlik application, and add the `iris_test` data to it. Now, we will add the `id` field into our test data. To do that, you can use the following code:

```
iris:
LOAD
RowNo() as id,
      sepal_length,
      sepal_width,
```

```
      petal_length,
      petal_width
FROM [lib://<PATH TO DATAFILE>/iris_test.csv]
(txt, utf8, embedded labels, delimiter is ',', msq);
```

> **Note**
>
> Our `iris_test.csv` dataset is randomly generated to mimic the characteristics of the
> original `iris` dataset and does not represent the actual data. It should be only used for
> demonstration purposes.

Now, we will create a connection to our deployed machine learning model. Select **Create new connection**
under the data connections, and then select **Qlik AutoML**. A view like the following will open:

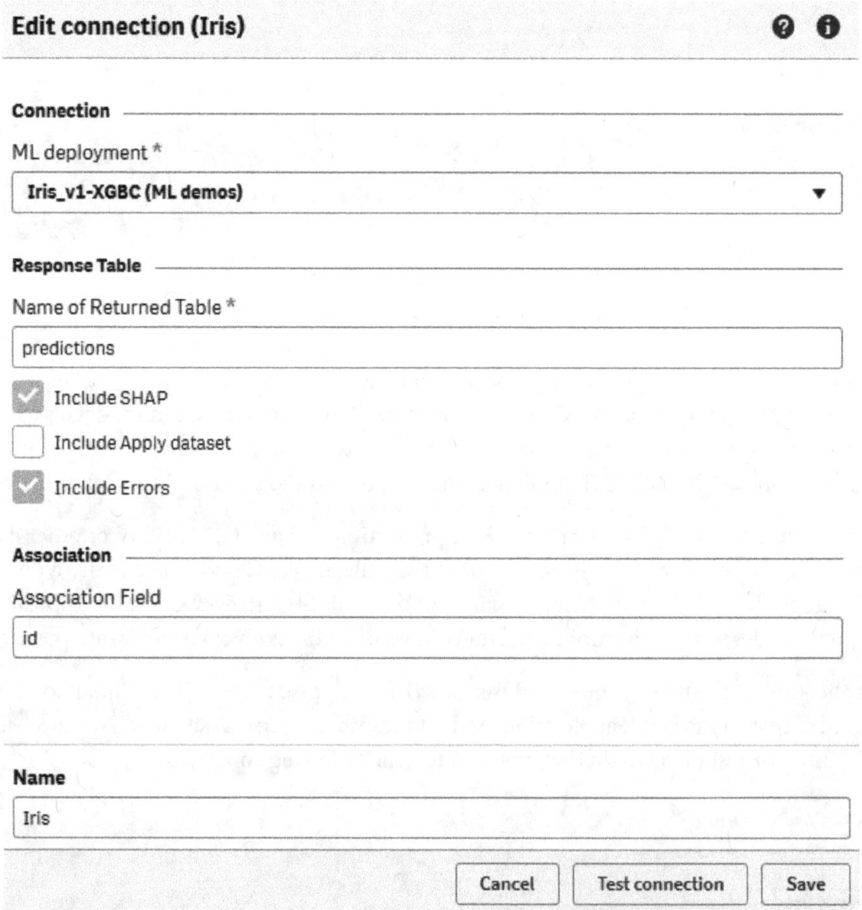

Figure 8.12: A data connection to the machine learning model

Select our deployed model from the **ML deployment** dropdown. Then, provide a name for the returned response table. In our example, it's called `predictions`. Select **Include SHAP** and **Include Errors**, since we want our result table to also include these columns. SHAP is not available for every algorithm, but it is a good practice to select it. If it's not available, it will not appear in the results table. In our case, these values are not available.

In **Association Field**, type `id`. This is a field that ties the generated predictions and our original data together. We generated the `id` field in our data earlier. Provide a name for your data connection, and click **Save**. You should see a new data connection appear in your application; let's use it. Click **Select data**, as shown in the following screenshot:

Figure 8.13: Select data in the AutoML connection

The data selection wizard will appear, as shown in the following screenshot:

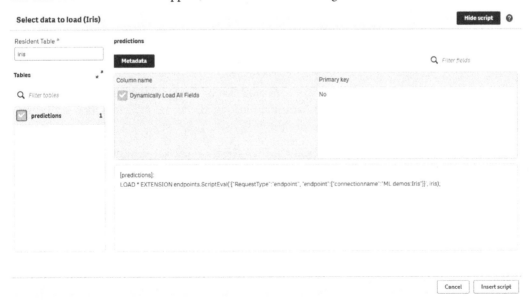

Figure 8.14: The data selection wizard

In the **Resident Table** field, type iris. This is our original dataset, which we will use to get predictions. Select the predictions table under the **Tables** section. This is our results table. There is no preview available, but you can see the script generated. Select **Insert script**. We can now see that our connector generated the following script:

```
[predictions]:
 LOAD * EXTENSION endpoints.ScriptEval('{"RequestType":"endpoint",
 "endpoint":{"connectionname":"ML demos:Iris"}}', iris);
```

Basically, our connector uses the API to send the iris table into our machine learning model and gets the prediction table back. It takes the connection name as a parameter and our data table (iris) as an input. We can now load our application and investigate the data model viewer. You should see a data model like the following:

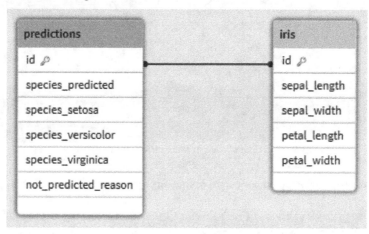

Figure 8.15: The data model

As we can see, our connector returned a predictions table that is connected to our original data table, using id as a key. The predictions table contains the actual prediction, a possible error message for each row, and the probability for every Iris species.

Now, we will investigate our prediction results further. Create a new sheet, and add the following elements to it:

- A filter pane, with all our features on the top.
- A scatter plot, with Avg(petal_width) on the *y* axis and Avg(petal_length) on the *x* axis and Id as a bubble. Color by dimension, and select species_predicted as the coloring dimension.
- A table containing all our features.

- A bar chart, with `Count (species_predicted)` as the bar height and `species_predicted` as the dimension.

- Four KPI objects that we will configure later.

- Four variable inputs, with text and an image container on the left side of each of them.

You should end up with a layout like the following:

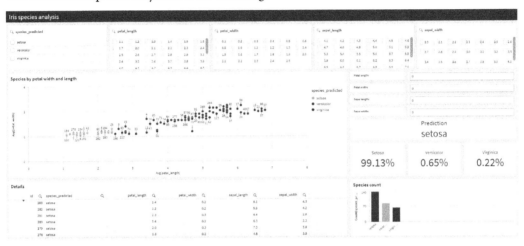

Figure 8.16: The application layout

> **Note**
>
> You can find the complete application in the GitHub repository for this book.

As you can see from the results, we have managed to predict the species with our model. If we look at the scatter plot, it seems that our model gives good results, keeping in mind that our data is randomly generated. As a last step, we will create a simulation that will utilize the API of our model.

We will start by creating the following variables:

```
v_sepal_length
v_sepal_width
v_petal_length
v_petal_width
```

Make 0 the default value for each variable. Since we have already created our variable input and labels, we can assign the variables into inputs and type the correct labels into place. You should end up with the following view:

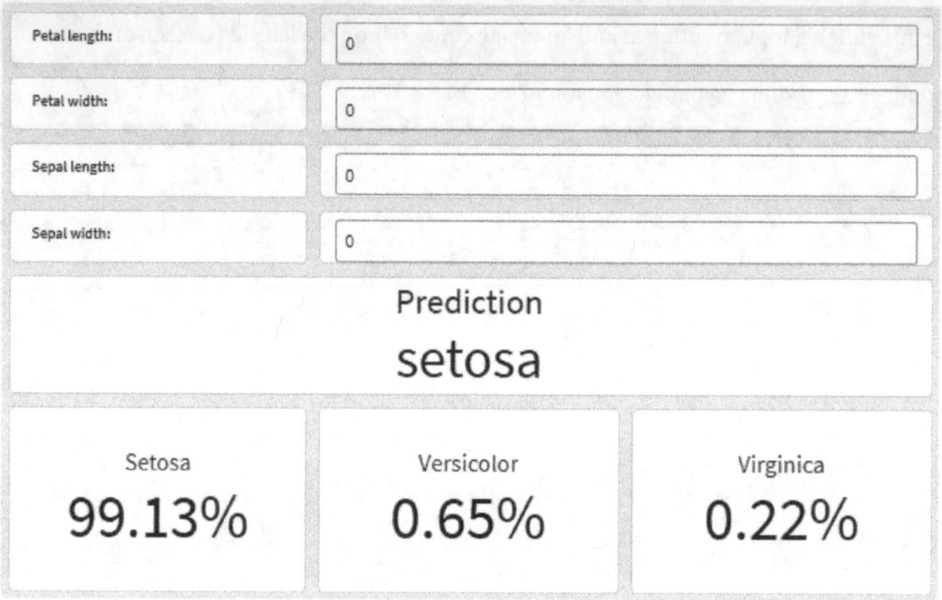

Petal length:	0
Petal width:	0
Sepal length:	0
Sepal width:	0

Prediction
setosa

Setosa	Versicolor	Virginica
99.13%	0.65%	0.22%

Figure 8.17: The simulation view

Now, we will set up the KPI objects. Select the first KPI, and type `Prediction` as a label. Enter the following formula in the **Expression** field:

```
=endpoints.ScriptEvalExStr('NNNN','{"RequestType":"endpoint",
"endpoint":{"connectionname":"ML demos:Iris","column":"species_
predicted"}}',
v_petal_length as petal_length,
v_petal_width as petal_width,
v_sepal_length as sepal_length,
v_sepal_width as sepal_width
)
```

This syntax might look familiar. We used the same principle in our earlier example with R. AutoML connector utilizes advanced analytics integration syntax.

With the advanced analytics integration, we have two sets of script functions:

- **ScriptEval**: After the hypercube has been aggregated, all rows in the specified columns are sent to the connector. The response expected is a single column. If multiple columns are returned, the first column that has the same number of rows as the input will be picked. The rows in the returned column must be in the same order as the input.

- **ScriptAggr**: Before the hypercube is aggregated, all rows for a single dimension group in the hypercube are sent, and the **server-side extension** (**SSE**) is expected to return a single one-column, one-row response. There will be one request sent to the SSE for each dimension value. While there are use cases for this, it is rare for this method to be used, as it can create performance issues if `ScriptAggr` is called with many dimensions.

For both the preceding sets, there are four different functions based on the data types:

- `ScriptEval(Script, Field 1, [Field n])`: The input fields and the response must be numeric.

- `ScriptEvalStr(Script, Field 1, [Field n])`: The input fields and the response must be a string.

- `ScriptEvalEx(DataTypes, Script, Field 1, [Field n])`: The input fields can be either string or numeric, the first parameter is a string of the datatypes, and the response must be numeric.

- `ScriptEvalExStr(DataTypes, Script, Field 1, [Field n])`: The input fields can be either string or numeric, the first parameter is a string of the datatypes, and the response must be string.

We used the `ScriptEvalExStr` function in the preceding example and defined the data types of our input fields, since they are numeric but the response is a string (`'NNNN'` for numerical fields).

Note that our script also contains the details of the connection to be used:

```
'{"RequestType":"endpoint", "endpoint":{"connectionname":"ML
demos:Iris","column":"species_predicted"}}'.
```

The connection name refers to the data connector that we created earlier. We have also determined the column that we want to get from the model. In our case, it is `species_predicted`. Selecting a correct return value is important. You can see all the possible fields – for example, from the data manager – if you have also used the model during the data load.

In the last part of our script, we will pass the variable values as input to our model. The names should match the names of our model schema. That's why we will use the `as` operator to rename the variables.

After configuring the KPI object, you should see `setosa` appear as a value. Since all our variables are defined to be 0, our model will give a prediction based on that information.

Add the following configurations to the three remaining KPI objects:

- **Label**: Setosa
- **Script**:

```
=endpoints.ScriptEvalEx('NNNN','{"RequestType":"endpoint",
"endpoint":{"connectionname":"ML demos:Iris","column":"species_
setosa"}}',
v_petal_length as petal_length,
v_petal_width as petal_width,
v_sepal_length as sepal_length,
v_sepal_width as sepal_width
)
```

- **Label**: Versicolor
- **Script**:

```
=endpoints.ScriptEvalEx('NNNN','{"RequestType":"endpoint",
"endpoint":{"connectionname":"ML demos:Iris","column":"species_
versicolor"}}',
v_petal_length as petal_length,
v_petal_width as petal_width,
v_sepal_length as sepal_length,
v_sepal_width as sepal_width
)
```

- **Label**: Virginica
- **Script**:

```
=endpoints.ScriptEvalEx('NNNN','{"RequestType":"endpoint",
"endpoint":{"connectionname":"ML demos:Iris","column":"species_
virginica"}}',
v_petal_length as petal_length,
v_petal_width as petal_width,
v_sepal_length as sepal_length,
v_sepal_width as sepal_width
)
```

As you might have noticed, the script is nearly the same in all our KPIs. We define the output by changing the value of the return column from the model. This way, we will get the probabilities for each species.

Try to modify the values in input fields, and you should get a prediction and probabilities for each of the species in real time.

We have now successfully finished the application and learned how to utilize Qlik AutoML in a cloud environment, using both load-time and real-time integration. In the following section, we will look at setting up an on-premises environment to integrate with Qlik AutoML.

Connecting Qlik AutoML to an on-premises environment

Qlik AutoML is a cloud tool that integrates tightly with a cloud tenant. However, it is possible to utilize the features from an on-premises environment. It is important to note that since Qlik AutoML still runs in a cloud environment, all data is also passed into the Qlik Cloud tenant. This approach is not suitable if the data can't leave the on-premises environment. The connection is encrypted and secure, and Qlik Cloud has all the major security certifications. It is also important to note that this approach will require a valid license for Qlik Cloud.

> **Note**
>
> More information about Qlik Cloud security and compliance is available at the Qlik Trust site: `https://www.qlik.com/us/trust`

We can see the basic architecture of integrating AutoML with an on-premises environment in the following diagram:

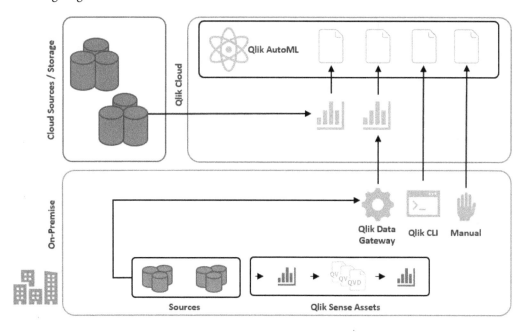

Figure 8.18: Qlik AutoML – on-premises and SaaS integration

In the preceding diagram, we have our on-premises environment at the bottom. We will handle most of the data loads in the on-premises environment in this architecture. After preparing a machine-learning-ready dataset, we can utilize Qlik Data Gateway, the Qlik CLI, or manually upload to a cloud tenant. This data can be supplemented using data coming from other cloud sources. When our training data is in the cloud, training the machine learning model will involve the same process from the previous section. It is also possible to automate the whole process using tasks, application automation, and the Qlik CLI. Once the model is trained, we can then utilize the prediction API directly from the on-premises environment.

Specific details about implementing the described environment are different in each organization. The preceding diagram can be used as a rough reference, but specific implementation should be planned case by case.

The goal of this section was to give some ideas about the usage of Qlik AutoML in hybrid scenarios. In the following section, we will investigate some of the best practices when working with Qlik AutoML.

Best practices with Qlik AutoML

There are some general guidelines and best practices when working with Qlik AutoML. Following these practices and principles will make it easier to get accurate results and handle the machine learning project flow. The general principles include the following:

- **Define the problem**: Clearly define the problem you are trying to solve with Qlik AutoML. Identify the variables you want to predict, and understand the available data. This is one of the most important best practices.

- **Prepare and clean the data**: Ensure that your data is in a format suitable for analysis. This may involve cleaning missing values, handling outliers, transforming variables, cleaning duplicates, and making sure the data is well formatted. This is typically the most time-consuming part of machine learning projects.

- **Feature engineering**: Explore and create meaningful features from your raw data. Qlik AutoML can automate some feature engineering tasks, but it's still important to understand your data and apply domain knowledge to generate relevant features.

- **Interpretability and explainability**: Understand and interpret the results of your models. Qlik AutoML provides tools to interpret generated models, and understands the contribution of different features to the predictions.

- **Validation and evaluation**: Use proper evaluation metrics to assess the performance of your models. Qlik AutoML can provide default metrics, but always cross-validate results when possible.

- **Monitoring and maintenance**: Continuously monitor the performance of your models in production. Update and retrain the models periodically as new data becomes available.

- **Iterative process**: Machine learning is an iterative process, so be prepared to refine and improve your models based on feedback and new insights.

Qlik AutoML is a powerful tool to build machine learning models in an automated way, and it can make it easier for end users to understand complex models. When utilizing the tool, and keeping in mind the basic principles described previously, organizations can get more out of their data. Remember that no machine learning tool is a magic box that can solve all the business problems in the world. The better you prepare the problem definition and training data, the more accurate results you will get from a model.

Summary

In this chapter, we discovered the usage of Qlik AutoML. We first learned what the tool will provide for users and what its key features are. We built our first machine learning model with Qlik AutoML using the famous Iris dataset. In this section, we discovered how to run experiments and deploy a model from experimentation. We also discovered how to utilize the model in a Qlik application, both during a data load and in real time. We learned from different metrics how our model performed.

In the latter part of this chapter, we took a quick look at an on-premises environment. We learned how to utilize Qlik AutoML in hybrid scenarios and how to set up our environment in these use cases. We also discovered some of the best practices to be used with Qlik AutoML.

In the following chapter, we will dive deep into data visualization. We will discover the techniques to visualize machine-learning-related data and investigate the use of some of the lesser-used graph types. We will also learn about common charts and visualizations, and we will discover some of the settings and configurations that will help us get the most out of our data.

9

Advanced Data Visualization Techniques for Machine Learning Solutions

In the rapidly evolving world of data analytics and machine learning, the ability to effectively visualize complex information has become crucial. As organizations strive to extract valuable insights from vast amounts of data, they need powerful tools that can transform raw numbers into meaningful visual representations.

In this chapter, we delve into the realm of advanced data visualization techniques within the context of machine learning solutions. We explore how Qlik's sophisticated visual analytics capabilities can enhance the understanding and interpretation of machine learning models and their outputs.

This chapter will equip you with the knowledge and skills necessary to effectively leverage Qlik's visual analytics capabilities to gain deeper insights, make informed decisions, and drive actionable outcomes in the era of machine learning and big data.

The main topics covered in this chapter are as follows:

- Visualizing machine learning data
- Chart and visualization types in Qlik

Visualizing machine learning data

When visualizing machine learning data, several important aspects should be considered to ensure effective communication and interpretation of the insights. The following should be considered (these are not tool-specific):

- **Understand the data**: Gain a deep understanding of the data you are working with. Analyze its structure, distributions, and relationships to identify key variables and patterns. This understanding will guide you in selecting appropriate visualization techniques.

- **Choose the right visualization techniques**: Select visualization techniques that best represent the characteristics and relationships within the data. Common techniques include scatter plots, line charts, bar charts, histograms, heatmaps, and network graphs. Choose techniques that effectively convey the information you want to communicate. In the next chapter, we will discover the different visualizations that Qlik offers.

- **Simplify and reduce complexity**: Keep the visualizations as simple and clear as possible. Avoid clutter and excessive detail, which can confuse the audience. Highlight the most important insights and use visual cues such as colors and annotations to guide the viewer's attention.

- **Use appropriate visual encodings**: Leverage visual encodings to represent different attributes of the data effectively. Utilize position, length, angle, color, size, and shape to encode variables and convey meaningful information. Make sure the chosen encodings accurately represent the data attributes.

- **Consider scaling and normalization**: If the data has a wide range of values or varying scales, consider scaling or normalizing the data to ensure accurate visualization. Scaling techniques such as standardization or min-max scaling can help bring data within a comparable range for proper visualization.

- **Utilize interactive visualizations**: Incorporate interactivity into your visualizations to enable users to explore the data dynamically. Allow for zooming, panning, filtering, and selecting data points of interest. Interactive visualizations enhance user engagement and understanding of the data. With Qlik tools, interaction is built in, so there is no need for extra steps.

- **Provide context and interpretation**: Include clear labels, titles, and axis descriptions to provide context and guide interpretation. Explain the meaning of the visualized data and provide relevant background information. Add captions, legends, or tooltips to help viewers understand the visual elements.

- **Consider multiple views or multiple visualizations**: Sometimes, presenting the data through multiple views or multiple visualizations can provide a more comprehensive understanding. Combine different techniques, such as overlaying multiple plots or using small multiples, to reveal different aspects of the data. In Qlik Sense, consider the structure of the application and how to utilize sheets to divide the data into informative views.

- **Test and iterate**: Test the visualizations with different users or stakeholders to gather feedback and improve their effectiveness. Iterate on the design based on user feedback and refine the visualizations to ensure they are clear, insightful, and meet the intended goals.

- **Tailor visualizations to the audience**: Consider the knowledge and expertise of your audience when designing visualizations. Adapt the level of detail, technicality, and complexity of the visualizations to the audience's understanding. Provide explanations and context as necessary.

One important aspect of any data visualization is the effective use of color. When designing a color scheme for the data visualization, the following aspects should be considered:

- **Choose a purposeful color palette**: Select a color palette that aligns with the purpose and context of the visualization. Consider using qualitative color schemes (distinct colors for different categories), sequential color schemes (gradation of colors for ordered data), or diverging color schemes (highlighting extremes or differences). You can use tools such as color pickers or online color palette generators to find harmonious and visually pleasing color combinations.

- **Differentiate categories**: When representing different categories or groups, use distinct colors to ensure clear differentiation. Avoid using similar hues that may cause confusion or make it difficult to distinguish between categories. Ensure that the chosen colors are visually distinguishable, even for individuals with color vision deficiencies.

- **Use color consistently**: Maintain consistency in the use of colors across the visualization. Assign the same color to the same category or variable throughout the visualization to provide visual continuity and aid interpretation. Consistency helps users establish mental associations between colors and the corresponding data elements.

- **Highlight key elements**: Utilize color to draw attention to important elements or highlight specific data points of interest. Use a contrasting or vibrant color for emphasis. For instance, you can highlight outliers, maximum and minimum values, or data points that meet specific criteria to make them visually stand out.

- **Consider color symbolism**: Be mindful of any inherent symbolism associated with colors in different cultures or contexts. Colors may have different connotations or meanings in different contexts. Consider cultural sensitivities and ensure that color choices do not unintentionally convey misleading or inappropriate messages.

- **Maintain accessibility**: Ensure that the chosen colors are accessible to a wide range of users, including those with color vision deficiencies. Avoid relying solely on color to convey information. Use alternative visual cues, such as patterns, labels, or textures, to supplement or replace color distinctions. Tools such as ColorBrewer and accessible color palette generators can help create color palettes that meet accessibility guidelines.

- **Balance the visual hierarchy**: Use colors to establish a visual hierarchy within the visualization. Employ different shades or intensities of a color to indicate varying levels of importance or significance. Lighter colors can be used for background or less important elements, while darker or bolder colors can be used for key elements or primary focus areas.

- **Limit the number of colors**: Avoid using too many colors in a single visualization, as it can lead to visual clutter and confusion. Limit the color palette to a manageable number of distinct colors based on the number of categories or variables being represented. Consider using additional visual encoding techniques such as size, shape, or texture to supplement color differentiations if necessary.

> **Note**
>
> Color themes and gradients for the Qlik application can be defined using themes or put them directly into the application. If there is a common color theme that should be used across multiple applications, a custom theme is recommended.

Now that we have learned some basic principles about data visualizations and colors, in the next section, we will take a closer look at some of the charts that Qlik Sense provides.

Chart and visualization types in Qlik

In this section, we will take a closer look at different visualization types in Qlik. We will also discover the general settings for layouts. As of writing this chapter, the following visualization types are supported (bolded ones are covered in more detail in this chapter):

Charts:

- **Bar charts**
- **Box plots**
- **Bullet charts**
- Combo charts
- **Distribution plots**
- Gauges
- **Histograms**
- Line charts
- **Maps**
- Pie charts

- **Scatter plots**
- Treemaps
- **Waterfall charts**

Text-based visualizations:

- Filter panes
- KPIs
- Pivot tables
- Tables
- Text & image

Dashboard objects:

- Buttons
- Containers

> **Note**
>
> In this chapter, we cover only the native visualizations available. There are also visualizations available in the Visualization bundle and the Dashboard bundle that include Qlik-supported extension objects. It is also possible to create fully custom visualization extensions or use the ones created by the community. These are, however, out of the scope of this book.

Bar charts

A bar chart is one of the most common visualization types. It is typically used to compare multiple values. The dimension axis represents the category items that are compared, and the measure axis shows the value of each item. Bar charts are particularly useful when working with discrete or categorical data. In a machine learning context, bar charts are typically used in feature analysis, model evaluation, or class distribution, for example. In our earlier Iris dataset example, we used a bar chart to represent the distribution of predicted Iris species. This chart looks as follows:

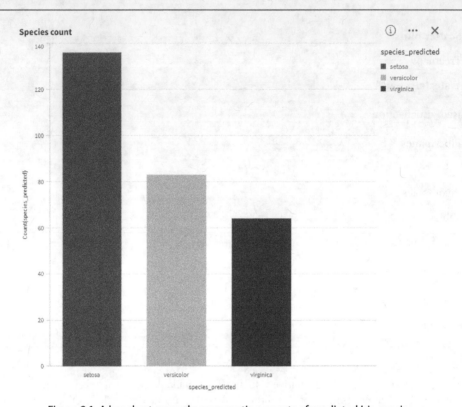

Figure 9.1: A bar chart example representing counts of predicted Iris species

This example represents a simple bar chart. More complex representations include grouped or stacked bars, where multiple categories can be represented at the same time. Grouped bars are good for comparison, while stacked bars can be used to visualize the relationships of subcategories that form a total.

For example, grouped bars can be used to compare the sales and forecasts of different years side by side, and stacked bars can be used to analyze the sales of different product categories. In this case, the total height of the bar is the total sales.

Box plots

Box plots, also known as box-and-whisker plots, are a valuable visualization tool for understanding the distribution and statistical properties of numerical data. Box plots are suitable for comparing ranges and distributions for groups of numerical data, which are illustrated with boxes and whiskers. Whiskers represent the high and low reference values. Box plots can organize a large amount of data and visualize outliers effectively. Typical use cases for box plots with machine learning data include data exploration, feature comparison, and outlier detection. The following example represents the box plot that shows the distribution of average petal length for the predicted species:

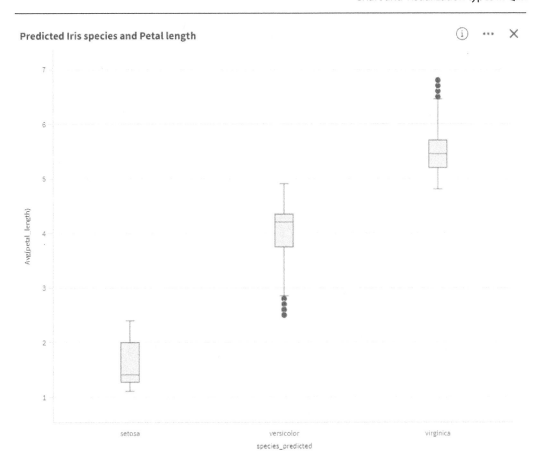

Figure 9.2: A box plot example visualizing the average petal length for the predicted species

In Qlik, you can select between the presets for the box plot or define the formula for each component on your own. In the previous graph, we can see that we have some outliers that extend beyond the whiskers, which are represented by the blue dots. We can see that the versicolor has the longest box and whiskers. This tells us that the species predicted to be versicolor in our model has the largest distribution of petal lengths measured. The mean petal length for each predicted species is marked by a horizontal line in each box.

Bullet charts

Bullet charts are powerful visualization tools that combine the features of a bar chart and a range chart. They provide a compact and informative representation of data, making them useful for comparing actual values against target values and displaying performance metrics. Bullet charts make it possible to compare and measure performance with enriched information. It is a good chart for comparing performance according to target. The following represents an example of a bullet chart:

Predicted Iris species and Petal length

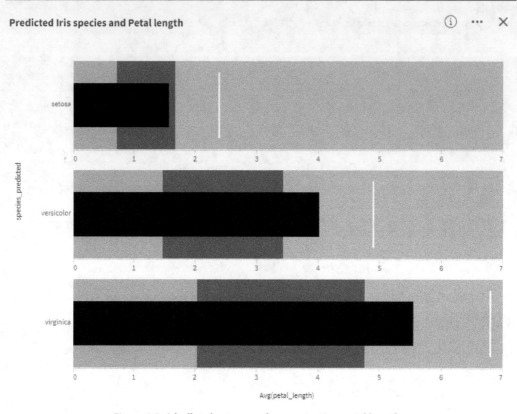

Figure 9.3: A bullet chart example representing petal lengths

In this example, we have set the maximum petal length as the target, visualized using a white vertical line. We have set the color scheme to represent the 30% and 70% marks to the target, and the black bar visualizes the average petal length for each iris species.

Distribution plots

A distribution plot, also known as a density plot, is a useful visualization for understanding the distribution of a numerical variable in a dataset. It displays the probability density of the data across different intervals or bins. With distribution plots, you can visually explore and understand the distributional properties of machine learning data. They provide insights into the shape, central tendency, and variability of numerical variables, aiding in data exploration, feature engineering, and model-building processes. A distribution plot is suitable for comparing ranges and distributions for groups of numerical data. An example can be seen in the following figure:

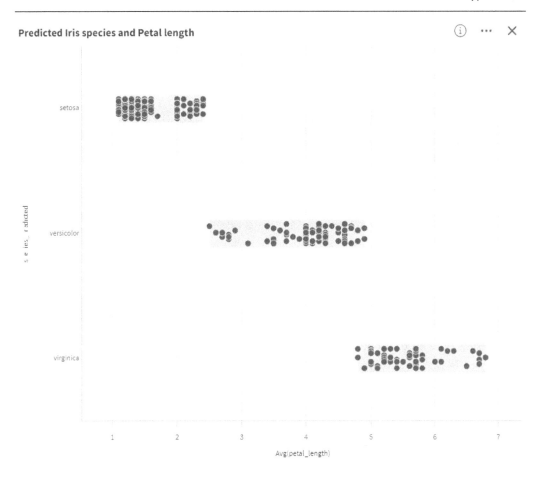

Figure 9.4: A distribution plot example representing petal length

In this graph, we can see that the individual measurements for petal length are marked with blue dots and the distributions of the measurements are marked with a gray background. We can easily see the construction of the data. In the graph, the bubble size parameter for individual measurements is adjusted to be smaller than the default size to get a clearer graph. If there are a lot of data points, it is also possible to enable jitter. This will separate the individual points using different vertical positions.

Histogram

Histograms are a common visualization technique used to represent the distribution of numerical data. They provide insights into the frequency or count of values within predefined intervals or bins. They are suitable for showing the distribution of numerical data over an interval or fixed period. Data is divided into bins, and each bar represents the frequency in each bin. In the following example, we are visualizing the frequency and distribution of house values in the California area:

House value distribution

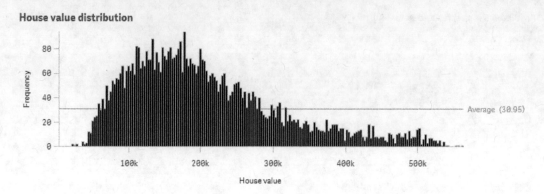

Figure 9.5: A histogram example visualizing the distribution of house values

In this example, we can see that the histogram is slightly tilted to the left. This tells us that most of the houses are valued between 100,000 USD and 300,000 USD, but there are still some houses that are more expensive than this. These form a long "tail" to the right. We can also see that, on average, each price bin has ~31 houses. In Qlik Sense, you can modify the number of bars and colors among many other parameters. In this example, the number of bars has been increased to 200 to get more accurate results from the distribution.

Maps

Maps in Qlik Sense are an extremely versatile visualization object that can be used in many ways. Maps can contain multiple layers and display different types of information on the same visualization. The best and most natural way to utilize maps is when the data is geography-based, but a map object can also be used to visualize data on top of different backgrounds, such as SVG images. Maps in Qlik support multiple coordinate systems and when combined with the GeoAnalytics Connector, you can perform further calculations with the data. The following example shows an example map with different visualizations:

House values on a map

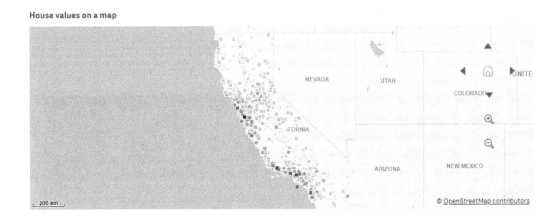

Figure 9.6: A map example with predicted house values plotted on a map with a gradient color scheme

This example visualizes the predicted house values in California on a map. Each point represents a house, and the color indicates the predicted value. A darker color means a house is more expensive. Heatmaps are useful for visualizing the density of the points on a map. In the following example, we have mapped the individual houses in a heatmap:

House density *

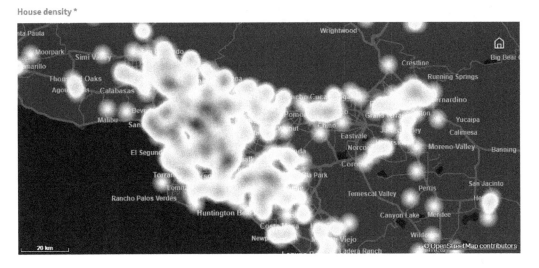

Figure 9.7: A heatmap example with individual houses plotted

The darker areas on a heatmap indicate a denser population of houses in that area. Combining different layers into visualizations is an extremely powerful way to present geographical data.

In the next example, we can see Tesla's supercharger stations in Norway that are located within a 300 km driving range along the road network. Driving ranges are calculated using the GeoAnalytics Connector and visualized on a map:

Travel areas and chargers

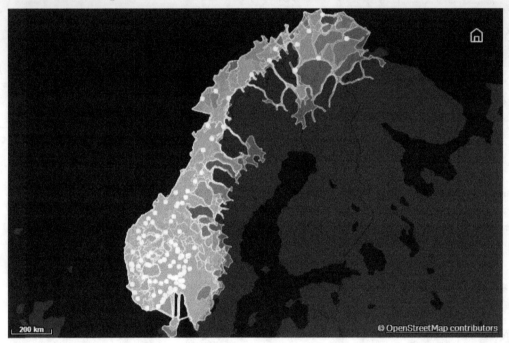

Figure 9.8: A map example showing 300 km driving range from each Tesla supercharger station in Norway

As the previous figures show, maps are powerful visualization objects, and they are highly recommended for use with geographical data. In many machine learning solutions, we can place the results onto a map.

Scatter plots

A scatter plot is a type of data visualization that displays the relationship between two numerical variables. It uses individual data points represented by dots on a two-dimensional plane, with one variable plotted on the x-axis and the other on the y-axis. Scatter plots can be used to help identify patterns, correlations, or outliers and assist in selecting features, identifying important variables, and understanding the behavior of the data. Scatter plots are also good for the cross-validation of the data and machine learning models. An example of a scatter plot using the Iris dataset can be seen in the following figure:

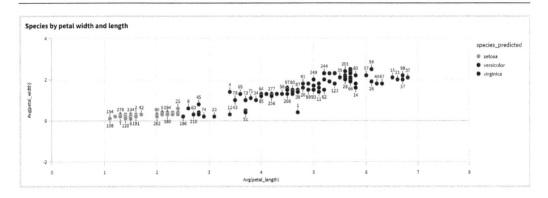

Figure 9.9: A scatter plot example of Iris species by petal width and length

In this example, we have plotted individual IDs of the Iris flower dataset, with petal width on the vertical axis and petal length on the horizontal axis. We then used the predicted species as a color. This way we can see clear patterns in our data.

Scatter plots are also a good visualization type if there are a lot of data points. It will automatically switch to a compressed view if the number of data points exceeds the maximum value. This value can be adjusted in the chart settings. An example of a compressed view is the following:

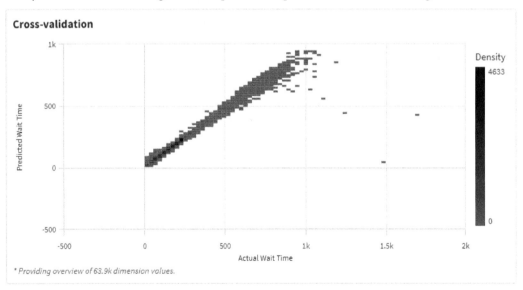

Figure 9.10: Scatter plot—compressed view

The compressed example visualizes the cross-validation of predicted waiting times in an ER unit compared to actual measured waiting times. Relation should be linear, but since we see some outliers, we know that there is still optimization to be done for our actual model in this case. The compressed view shows 64,000 data points in our example graph.

Waterfall charts

A waterfall chart is a visual representation of how various factors contribute to a final value. They help in understanding the cumulative effect of positive and negative changes in a dataset. While waterfall charts are commonly used in financial analysis, they can also be useful for analyzing and interpreting machine learning data. Waterfall charts are useful when visualizing the SHAP values for a Qlik AutoML model to learn how individual characteristics affect the predicted value. The following example represents the SHAP values of the California housing dataset:

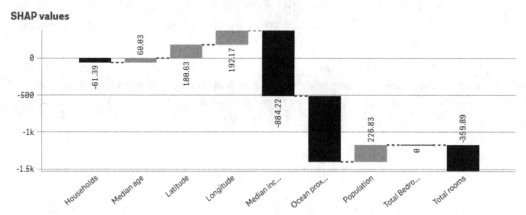

Figure 9.11: A waterfall chart example—SHAP values

In this example, we can see that Median income and Ocean proximity have large effects on the predicted value. The overall effects of these features are negative, but if we investigate the top predicted prices, we can see that the effect for this group is positive. This is described in the following figure:

SHAP values

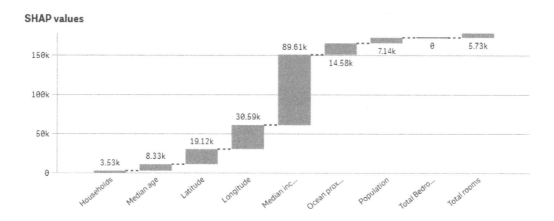

Figure 9.12: SHAP values visualized and filtered for houses with predicted prices over 300,000 USD

This way, we can study how the different variables are affecting predictions and model behavior. A waterfall chart is a good choice for this specific case since it easily visualizes how various factors contribute to a final value.

> **Note**
>
> We will cover the full hands-on example using California housing prices data in the next chapter.

Choosing visualization type

When it comes to visualizing data, a key goal is to present relationships and patterns effectively so that insights can be quickly gleaned. Qlik Sense provides a diverse set of visualizations and charts to cater to various data visualization needs. Each chart has its own strengths in representing data in distinct ways that can be tailored for different analytical purposes.

When choosing the appropriate chart for your data, it is crucial to consider the specific insights you aim to derive. Understanding what you want to visualize and the story you want to tell is vital in selecting the most suitable chart type. Different charts emphasize different aspects of the data, such as trends, comparisons, distributions, or relationships.

Qlik Sense offers a wide range of visualization options. Each chart type has unique characteristics and functionalities that cater to specific data analysis requirements. For instance, bar charts are effective for comparing categorical data, while line charts are useful for visualizing trends over time. Scatter plots are ideal for showcasing relationships between two variables, and treemaps can effectively illustrate hierarchical data structures.

By carefully selecting the right chart types in Qlik Sense, you can leverage the strengths of each visualization to gain meaningful insights from your data. Understanding your data and the questions you want to answer will help you make informed decisions on which charts to utilize to present your data accurately and facilitate data-driven decision-making.

In the previous section, we covered some uncommon visualization types with examples and learned why these charts are good for visualizing machine-learning-related data. We did not cover all the charts, and there are a lot of options for tuning all the charts available. The best way to get familiar with different options is to play with the charts yourself. In the next chapter, we will build a few machine learning use cases from scratch and cover some of the chart settings while doing that.

Summary

Visualizing machine learning data is a crucial step in the data analysis process, enabling you to gain insights, identify patterns, and communicate results effectively. In this chapter, we familiarized ourselves with the different visualizations and techniques to visualize machine learning data. At the beginning of this chapter, we discovered common principles for creating a good visualization and familiarized ourselves with the key principles of coloring.

Toward the end of the chapter, we discovered some different visualization types that Qlik offers natively and learned how to use some of the graph types effectively. We learned the principles of the most used visualizations and how to fine-tune these in Qlik while keeping the context of machine learning in mind.

In the next chapter, we will look at the actual use cases of the machine learning solutions. We will learn how to build a few different machine learning models and applications from scratch and utilize all we have learned from previous chapters.

Part 3:
Case studies and
best practices

This section will cover different use cases with hands-on examples. Use cases are built from scratch including the problem definition phase. The result is a working analytics application that utilizes machine learning. This section will provide the possibility to utilize all the skills learned from previous chapters. The section also covers the current and future trends of machine learning and AI and focuses on the characteristics of megatrends.

This section has the following chapters:

- *Chapter 10: Examples and Case Studies*
- *Chapter 11: Future Direction*

10

Examples and Case Studies

This chapter embarks on a journey into the realm of machine learning, exploring practical applications and real-world examples that demonstrate its power and potential. In the previous chapters, we have learned all the essential skills required to build a good machine learning solution. In this chapter, we will utilize all the knowledge gained and build the following examples from scratch:

- Linear regression example
- Customer churn example

Linear regression example

In this example, we will create a linear regression model to predict the value of a house in the California area. Let's begin by getting familiar with the dataset. We will use a common California house values dataset. This is a collection of data related to residential real estate properties in various regions of California, USA. It is commonly used in machine learning and data analysis tasks for predicting house prices based on various features.

The dataset we will use contains the following fields:

- `medianIncome`: The median income of households in a specific block.
- `housingMedianAge`: The median age of houses in a block.
- `totalRooms`: The total number of rooms in the houses in a block.
- `totalBedrooms`: The total number of bedrooms in the houses in a block.
- `population`: The total population of the block.
- `households`: The total number of households (a group of people residing within a home unit) within a block.
- `latitude`: The latitude of the geographical location of the house.
- `longitude`: The longitude of the geographical location of the house.

- `medianHouseValue`: The median value of houses in the block.

- `oceanProximity`: Categorical description of the distance to the ocean

Here is a sample of the data:

longitude	latitude	housing_median_age	total_rooms	total_bedrooms	population	households	median_income	median_house_value	ocean_proximity
-116.46	33.82	6	4863	920	3010	828	3.9508	104200	INLAND
-117.04	34	21	4624	852	2174	812	3.5255	132100	INLAND
-121.03	37.55	32	946	198	624	173	1.9728	97900	INLAND
-117.8	33.68	8	2032	349	862	340	6.9133	274100	<1H OCEAN
-122.26	37.83	52	1656	420	718	382	2.6768	182300	NEAR BAY
-118.99	35.39	52	2805	573	1325	522	2.5083	70100	INLAND
-122.35	37.96	29	1899	524	1357	443	1.875	97200	NEAR BAY
-117.9	33.66	13	1642	423	841	368	3.6042	226000	<1H OCEAN
-117.05	32.75	43	1718	344	826	336	2.7014	133700	NEAR OCEAN
-117.2	34.5	10	4201	850	2378	808	2.1781	92200	INLAND
-118.85	34.25	17	5593	732	1992	660	7.2965	342900	<1H OCEAN
-121.96	37.27	31	3347	589	1566	597	5.5151	286800	<1H OCEAN
-122.08	37.36	31	2717	376	1001	381	9.281	500001	NEAR BAY

Figure 10.1: Sample data from a California housing dataset

> **Note**
>
> The example dataset can be found in the GitHub repository of this book. A good place to find other datasets is, for example, `https://www.kaggle.com/datasets`.

The first step in our machine learning project is to define a question we want to answer using our model. In this case, we are using a rather simple historical dataset and therefore the framework used is modified a bit. Let's determine the following characteristics to start:

- **Trigger**: A new house data is inserted into the dataset

- **Target**: The value of the house in US dollars

- **Features**: Latitude, longitude, median age, total rooms, total bedrooms, population, households, median income, ocean proximity

- **Machine learning question**: Predicting what will the house value be in the California area?

To begin our actual work, let's first upload `housing_test.csv` and `housing_train.csv` into our Qlik cloud tenant. These files can be found in the GitHub repository of this book. As you can see, the dataset is already split into train and test datasets.

In a normal machine learning project, we would need to take care of encoding the categorical fields, handling null values, scaling and so on, but in our case, Qlik AutoML takes care of all these steps. Our next task is to create a new machine learning experiment (**Add New → New ML Experiment**).

Give a name to your experiment, define a space you want to use, and press **Create**. The first step to starting our new experiment is to define the dataset used. Select `housing_train.csv`, which we uploaded earlier. You should see the following:

Figure 10.2: Housing prices experiment – target selection

Next, we will select our target variable. We can also select the features to be used in our experiment. Select `median_house_value` as the target and all other fields should be automatically selected to be included in our experiment. You should see something like the following:

	Feature	Data type	Feature type	Distinct values	Null values	Sample values / Stats	Insights
☑	longitude	Float (Double)	Numeric ⌄	808	0	-118.3 (116), -118.31 (113), -118.29 (107)	
☑	latitude	Float (Double)	Numeric ⌄	826	0	34.06 (176), 34.05 (169), 34.07 (160)	
☑	housing_median_age	Integer	Numeric ⌄	52	0	52 (875), 35 (598), 36 (584)	
☑	total_rooms	Integer	Numeric ⌄	5251	0	1527 (14), 1613 (13), 2127 (12)	
☑	total_bedrooms	String	Numeric ⌄	1768	0	NaN (138), 346 (37), 331 (36)	ⓘ Impact encoded
☑	population	Integer	Numeric ⌄	3532	0	1005 (20), 825 (18), 837 (18)	
☑	households	Integer	Numeric ⌄	1666	0	426 (40), 429 (40), 340 (39)	
☑	median_income	Float (Double)	Numeric ⌄	9865	0	2.625 (35), 15.0001 (32), 2.875 (32)	
◎	median_house_value	Integer	Numeric ⌄	3547	0	500001 (681), 137500 (85), 162500 (84)	
☑	ocean_proximity	String	Categorical ⌄	5	0	<1H OCEAN (6419), INLAND (4545), NEAR OCEAN (1884)	ⓘ One-hot encoded

Figure 10.3: Target and features selected

In the previous image, we have also marked the feature type of `total_bedrooms` with a red square. Qlik has recognized this field as a string and forms a categorical feature by default. Change that to **Numeric** using the small arrow sign on the field. Once you have done the target selection and changed the feature type for `total_bedrooms`, we can select **Run Experiment** from the bottom right corner. After a while, you should see the following:

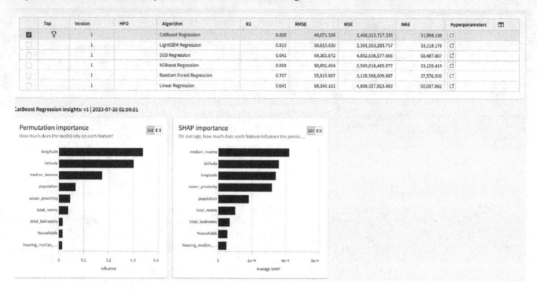

Figure 10.4: Housing prices experiment – first results

When looking at the SHAP diagrams for our first version of the experiment, we can see that the `median_income` field has a rather high correlation with the predicted house values. Let's try to configure a second version of our experiment without that field.

Select **Configure v2** from the lower right corner. A panel similar to what we saw during our initial configuration will show up. Under the **Features** tab, deselect `median_income` as in the following figure:

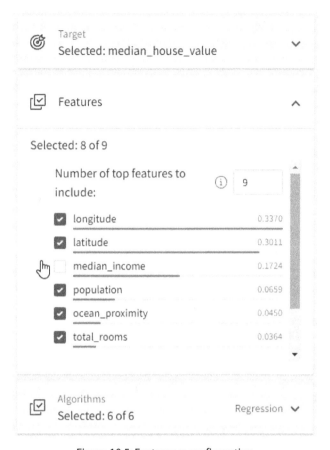

Figure 10.5: Features reconfiguration

Select **Run v2** and you should see updated SHAP and Permutation importance graphs after the experiment has finished. We can now see that total_rooms is the most determining feature, but our R2 score has also dropped. In this case, we will go with the first version of our experiment since it gave us better accuracy. You can try to configure multiple versions and experiment with the models to get a better model.

In the list at the top part of the screen, scroll down until you see the top-performing model of the first run and select it. Your screen should look like the following:

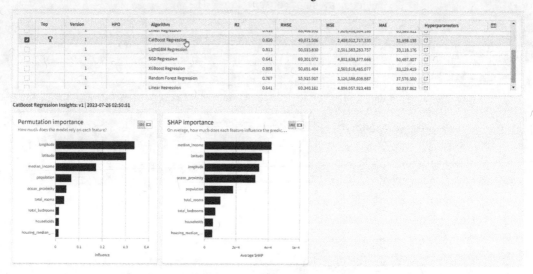

Figure 10.6: The model selected for deployment.

Select **Deploy** from the bottom right corner. Enter a name and define the space for your newly deployed model. Make sure that **Enable real-time API access** is selected and press **Deploy**. Our model is now deployed and ready for use.

As we have learned in previous chapters, the deployed model itself provides information about the required schema, algorithm deployed, and some metadata from the experiment. You can open the deployed model and have a closer look at this information at this point.

Our next task to get the predicted results into a finalized application is to create a new Qlik analytics application.

For the data in our application, we will import `housing_test.csv`. After that, we will create a new data connection for the Qlik AutoML model that we deployed in the earlier step.

Create a new Qlik AutoML connection under **Data connections**. From the **ML deployment** field, select the model deployed earlier from the drop-down menu. Select the SHAP-values and errors to be included in the returned dataset and set the **Association Field** to `Id`. The connector settings should look similar to the following:

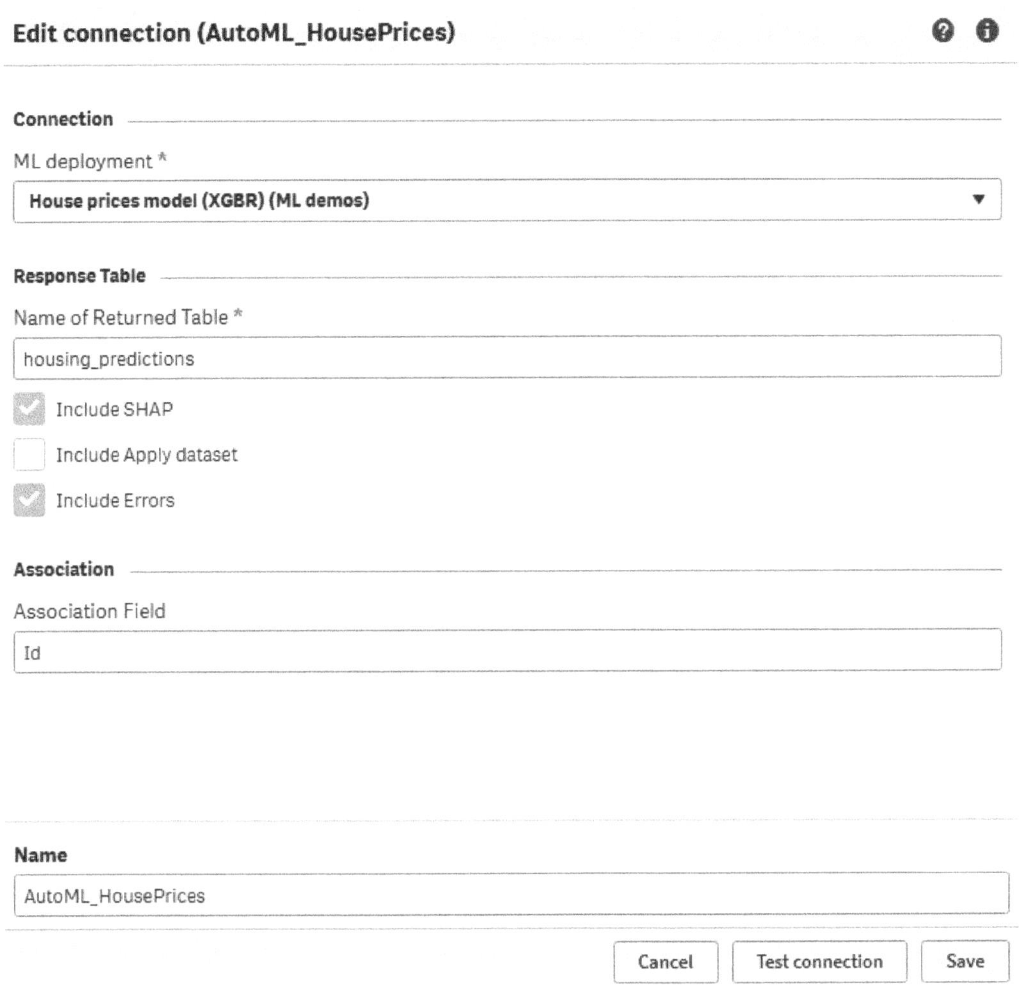

Edit connection (AutoML_HousePrices)   ❓ ⓘ

Connection ————————————————————————————————————

ML deployment *

| House prices model (XGBR) (ML demos) | ▼ |

Response Table —————————————————————————————————

Name of Returned Table *

| housing_predictions |

☑ Include SHAP

☐ Include Apply dataset

☑ Include Errors

Association ————————————————————————————————————

Association Field

| Id |

Name

| AutoML_HousePrices |

                              Cancel   Test connection   Save

Figure 10.7: Connector settings

Test the connection and save it after that. Next, we will select the data to load. In the **Resident Table** field, insert the name of the table containing our `housing_test.csv` and select `housing_predictions` to be included. You should see the following:

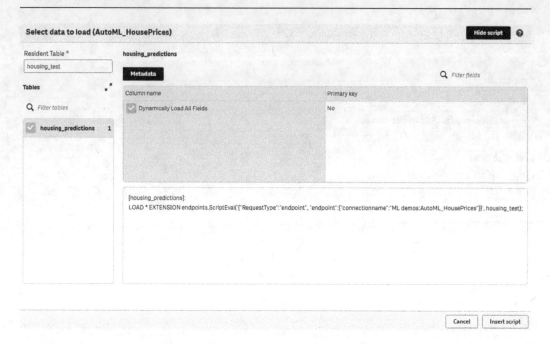

Figure 10.8: The Select data to load window.

Select **Insert script** and load the data into the application. You are now ready to create the actual dashboard.

> **Note**
>
> If you run into problems during the application creation, there is a sample application in the Github repository of this book for your reference.

We will not cover the dashboard creation part in detail to give you a chance to play with the different visualization options. The following image represents a sample dashboard that shows predicted house values on a map using a gradient color scheme, a histogram to show the distribution of prices, and a waterfall diagram to visualize SHAP values. Use the skills acquired from previous chapters and create a dashboard of your own to visualize the data.

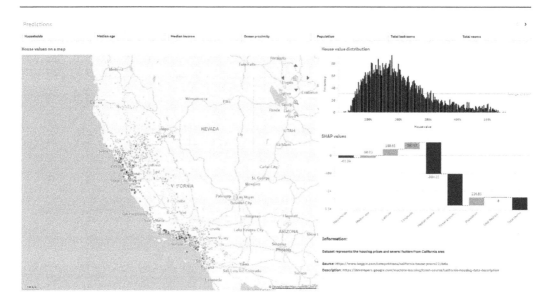

Figure 10.9: Housing prices – sample dashboard

You can create multiple dashboards and try to cross-reference the data from multiple models if you re-run the experiment with different parameters. Try to play with the different settings and graph types to find an effective visualization.

Now that we have implemented a linear regression example, it is time to move on to another example with a slightly more complex scenario. We will investigate the customer churn example next.

Customer churn example

In our second example, we will create a binary model to predict customer churn for a bank. We are going to use a dataset that contains the following fields:

- `customer_id`: A unique identifier for each customer.
- `credit_score`: A numerical representation of a customer's creditworthiness.
- `country`: The country where the customer resides.
- `gender`: The gender of the customer.
- `age`: The age of the customer.
- `tenure`: The duration of the customer's relationship with the company.
- `balance`: The current balance in the customer's account.
- `products_number`: The number of products the customer has brought from the company.

- **credit_card**: A binary indicator showing whether the customer holds a credit card with the company.

- **active_member**: A binary indicator indicating whether the customer is currently an active member of the company.

- **estimated_salary**: An approximate estimation of the customer's salary.

- **churn**: A binary indicator showing whether the customer has churned (1) or not (0). Churning refers to customers who have ended their relationship with the company.

Here is a sample of the dataset:

customer_id	credit_score	country	gender	age	tenure	balance	products_number	credit_card	active_member	estimated_salary	churn
15634602	619	France	Female	42	2	0	1	1	1	101348.9	1
15647311	608	Spain	Female	41	1	83807.86	1	0	1	112542.6	0
15619304	502	France	Female	42	8	159660.8	3	1	0	113931.6	1
15701354	699	France	Female	39	1	0	2	0	0	93826.63	0
15737888	850	Spain	Female	43	2	125510.8	1	1	1	79084.1	0
15574012	645	Spain	Male	44	8	113755.8	2	1	0	149756.7	1
15592531	822	France	Male	50	7	0	2	1	1	10062.8	0
15656148	376	Germany	Female	29	4	115046.7	4	1	0	119346.9	1
15792365	501	France	Male	44	4	142051.1	2	0	1	74940.5	0
15592389	684	France	Male	27	2	134603.9	1	1	1	71725.73	0
15767821	528	France	Male	31	6	102016.7	2	0	0	80181.12	0
15737173	497	Spain	Male	24	3	0	2	1	0	76390.01	0
15632264	476	France	Female	34	10	0	2	1	0	26260.98	0

Figure 10.10: Customer churn – sample data

To start with our machine learning project, we will first upload `Bank Customer Churn Prediction.csv` into Qlik Cloud. This data file can be found in the GitHub repository of this book. We also must split the dataset. Qlik AutoML splits the dataset during the experiment phase, but we will also create separate training and test datasets to get a better understanding of the model's performance. To split the dataset, we will use the training and test data in a ratio of 70:30.

Splitting the dataset can be done in Qlik. To do that, we will first create a new analytics application and name it `Churn Data Prep`. Next, create a data connection to the location that contains the previously uploaded `Bank Customer Churn Prediction.csv` file. You can use the following code to do the splitting:

```
banking_churn_data:
LOAD
    RowNo() as row,
    customer_id,
    credit_score,
    country,
    gender,
    "age",
    tenure,
    balance,
```

```
    products_number,
    credit_card,
    active_member,
    estimated_salary,
    churn
FROM [lib://<connection>/Bank Customer Churn Prediction.csv]
(txt, codepage is 28599, embedded labels, delimiter is ',', msq);
banking_churn_train:
NoConcatenate Load *
Resident banking_churn_data
Where row <= (NoOfRows('banking_churn_data')*0.7);
banking_churn_test:
NoConcatenate Load *
Resident banking_churn_data
Where row > (NoOfRows('banking_churn_data')*0.7);
drop Fields row From banking_churn_train, banking_churn_test;
Store banking_churn_train into [lib:// <connection>/banking_churn_
train.qvd] (qvd);
Store banking_churn_test into [lib:// <connection>/banking_churn_test.
qvd] (qvd);
```

The preceding code reads `Bank Customer Churn.csv` using the file data connection and adds a row number to each row. Then, two subsets (training and test) are created using this row number and are stored in QVD files. The `Row number` field is dropped before storing because we don't need it in our machine learning project. As a result of the script, the new data files (`banking_churn_train.qvd` and `banking_churn_test.qvd`) are stored in the same location as the original data file.

Next, we will start to investigate the data to form a machine learning question. Data exploration can be done in the same Qlik application where you split the data. Remember to drop the test and train tables before continuing with the visualizations. An example of an analysis view is represented in the following figure:

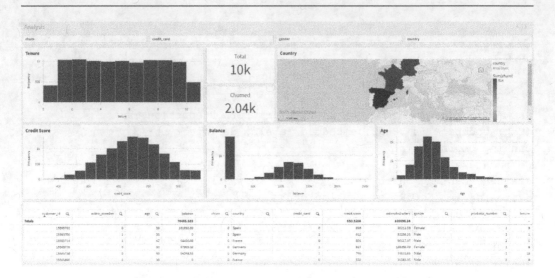

Figure 10.11: Customer churn example - Initial analysis

If we plot the values using a histogram, we can see that `credit_score` and `age` follow a normal distribution. If we look at the balance, there are lot of zero values, but the rest of the data is normally distributed. If we look at the tenure, there are only a few customers with 1 year of tenure and 95 of those have been churned. This is important information when defining our prediction window. We can also see that there are no issues in the data. You can play with different visualizations when getting familiar with the data. An example can be found in the GitHub repository of this book.

After investigating the data, we can use the following framework to form our machine learning question:

- **Event trigger**: When a new customer subscribes
- **Target**: When a customer leaves the company services (churn)
  - Binary outcome: Yes or No
  - The horizon is based on the average churned customer tenure length (around five years)
- **Features**: `active_member`, `age`, `balance`, `country`, `credit_card`, `credit_score`, `estimated_salary`, `gender`, `products_number`, and `tenure`
- **Prediction point**: One year after subscription
- **Machine learning question**: After one year of activity as a customer, will the customer churn during the first five years?

By defining our model using the framework, we have defined that after a new customer has signed, we will collect data during the first year and then predict whether the customer will churn during the first five years. We can re-calculate the predictions periodically after the initial results when we get new data (for example, every six months after the initial results). Since we had a minimal number of customers that churned during the first year, our data accumulation window (the time between the event trigger and the prediction point) is not too long.

Let's now create the actual machine learning experiment using our training dataset. Start by creating a new experiment and select the correct dataset (`banking_churn_train.qvd`). Select `churn` as the target and all the other fields except `customer_id` as features. The following figure represents the first experiment setup:

	Feature	Data type	Feature type		Distinct values	Null values	Sample values / Stats	Insights
	customer_id	Integer	Numeric	∨	7000	0	15634602 (1), 15647311 (1), 15619304 (1), 15701354 (1), 15737888 (1)	
☑	credit_score	Integer	Numeric	∨	451	0	850 (167), 655 (40), 652 (38), 667 (37), 705 (37)	
☑	country	String	Categorical	∨	3	0	France (3519), Spain (1750), Germany (1731)	ⓘ One-hot encoded
☑	gender	String	Categorical	∨	2	0	Male (3791), Female (3209)	ⓘ One-hot encoded
☑	age	Integer	Numeric	∨	69	0	37 (350), 38 (335), 35 (332), 33 (312), 36 (299)	
☑	tenure	Integer	Numeric	∨	11	0	7 (726), 8 (725), 3 (724), 2 (721), 1 (720)	
☑	balance	Float (Double)	Numeric	∨	4468	0	0 (2532), 130170.82 (2), 83807.86 (1), 159660.8 (1), 125510.82 (1)	
☑	products_number	Integer	Numeric	∨	4	0	1 (3593), 2 (3174), 3 (191), 4 (42)	
☑	credit_card	Integer	Numeric	∨	2	0	1 (4923), 0 (2077)	
☑	active_member	Integer	Numeric	∨	2	0	1 (3585), 0 (3415)	
☑	estimated_salary	Float (Double)	Numeric	∨	6999	0	24924.92 (2), 101348.88 (1), 112542.58 (1), 113931.57 (1), 93826.63 (1)	
⊚	churn	Integer	Numeric	∨	2	0	0 (5557), 1 (1443)	

Figure 10.12: Experiment setup

We can see that Qlik AutoML recognized the categorical features and will automatically apply one-hot encoding to these fields. You can now run the experiment. After the first run, the experiment returns the following results:

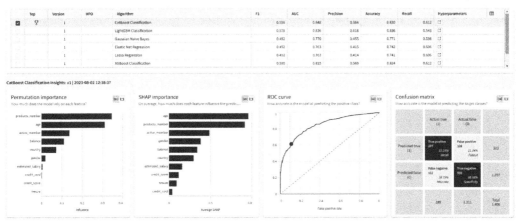

Figure 10.13: First results from the experiment

As we can see from the confusion matrix, the rate of false negatives is quite large and our ROC curve indicates that our model is not performing well. From the permutation and SHAP importance graphs we can see that `age` and `products_number` correlate highly with the result. Let's try to make another run without these variables and see if we will get more accurate results. Select **Configure v2** from the lower right corner. Under the **Features** panel, deselect `age` and `products_number` and press **Run v2**. You should see the following results:

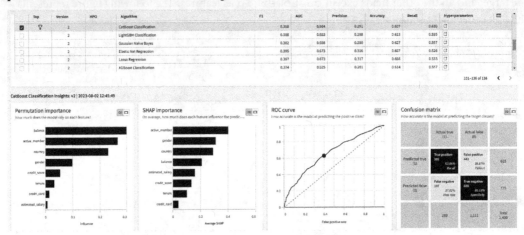

Figure 10.14: Results after modification

As we can see, the accuracy of the model dropped so our changes were not beneficial. After a few iterations, we will find the best combination of features. After that, it is possible to finetune the model even more by enabling hyperparameter optimization from the settings and defining a time window for that. You can try different combinations and investigate the model performance. Once you are done, configure the new version and select the following fields: `age`, `products_number`, `active_member`, `gender`, `balance`, and `country`. Also, enable hyperparameter optimization and set the window to one hour. You should see the following results:

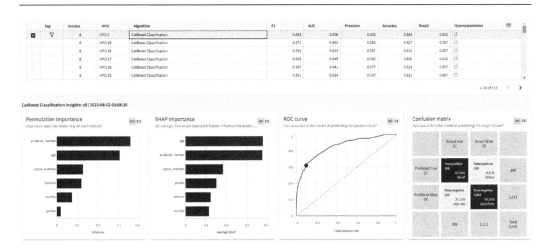

Figure 10.15: Results from the optimized experiment

We can see that the accuracy of our final model is 84.4% and the F1 score is 0.623. The model is not a top performer but will give us relatively good results. Select the top-performing model and press **Deploy**. This will create a machine learning deployment for us. You can open the deployed model. Verify that you see the following schema:

Model schema	
Training dataset **banking_churn_train**	
Feature	**Feature type**
country	Categorical
gender	Categorical
balance	Numeric
age	Numeric
products_number	Numeric
active_member	Numeric

Figure 10.16: Banking churn schema

We can now create a new analytics application and load `banking_churn_test.qvd` into it as a data table. You should do this in script view. We should also create a data connection to our newly deployed model. To create the correct data connection, select Qlik AutoML from the connection list and select the model from the dropdown menu. Give a name to the returned table and select SHAP -values and errors to be included. Type `customer_id` into **Association Field**. Your settings should look similar to the following:

Edit connection (Banking churn)   ❓ ⓘ

Connection ──────────────────────────────────────

ML deployment *

| Banking exp_v8-CATBC (ML demos)   ▼ |

Response Table ───────────────────────────────────

Name of Returned Table *

| churn_predicted |

☑ Include SHAP

☐ Include Apply dataset

☑ Include Errors

Association ───────────────────────────────────────

Association Field

| customer_id |

Name

| Banking churn |

                          Cancel   Test connection   Save

Figure 10.17: Connection settings

Next, add the predictions to the script. Enter the name of the `banking_churn_test` table into the **Resident Table** field and select the result set. Select **Insert script**. Your code should look as follows:

```
banking_churn_test:
LOAD
    customer_id,
    credit_score,
    country,
    gender,
    "age",
    tenure,
    balance,
```

```
      products_number,
      credit_card,
      active_member,
      estimated_salary,
      churn
FROM [lib://ML demos:DataFiles/banking_churn_test.qvd]
(qvd);
[churn_predicted]:
LOAD * EXTENSION endpoints.ScriptEval('{"RequestType":"endpoint",
"endpoint":{"connectionname":"ML demos:Banking churn"}}', banking_
churn_test);
```

We will load the test dataset in the preceding code, and then call the model endpoint through the data connector. After you complete the script, select **Load data**. Open **Data model viewer** and verify that you can see two tables connected. Next, we will focus on creating the actual application. You should try different visualization types and connect to the model using the **server-side extension** (**SSE**) syntax. An example dashboard may look like the following:

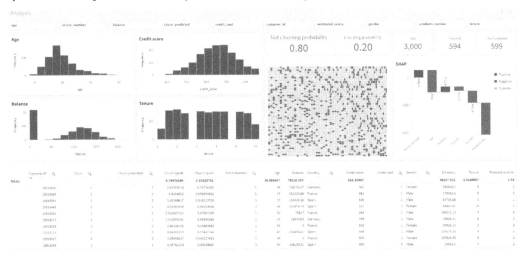

Figure 10.18: Churn analysis example

We will not cover the creation of every visualization in this chapter since you should experiment with the data and visualizations. A sample application is provided as part of the materials in the GitHub repository. We have now successfully implemented two different machine learning solutions with different use cases and studied how to form a machine learning question to be answered. We have also learned how to optimize and finetune a model.

Summary

In this chapter, we utilized the skills learned during the previous chapters by implementing two different use cases. In our first example, we studied the data of houses in California and created a model to predict their prices based on house-related variables. We created an application to utilize our model and learned about the iterations and how to interpret the experiment results.

In our second example, we learned how to form a customer churn model and utilize it in multiple ways. We also learned how to create different datasets from our original data file and how to form a machine learning question using a framework. We visualized the results using native visualizations in Qlik Sense.

In our next and last chapter, we will look into the future. We will investigate current trends in machine learning and artificial intelligence and try to predict how these might evolve in the future. We will also investigate megatrends and get familiar with the characteristics of a megatrend. We will also think about the evaluation of possible megatrends. Understanding megatrends is a crucial skill in being able to compete and evolve.

11
Future Direction

In the vast landscape of technological advancements, few innovations have captivated the world's imagination and transformed industries as profoundly as machine learning and **artificial intelligence (AI)**. These groundbreaking fields have the power to reshape our societies, revolutionize the way we work, and fundamentally alter the course of human existence. As we stand on the precipice of a new era, this chapter aims to explore the future of machine learning and AI, unraveling the intricacies of these technologies and envisioning their potential impact on various aspects of our lives.

In this chapter, we will look at the current and future trends in machine learning and AI. We will also learn the life cycle of megatrends and how to read them.

In this chapter, we will learn about the following topics:

- The future trends of machine learning and AI
- How to recognize potential megatrends

The future trends of machine learning and AI

Machine learning, a subfield of AI, empowers computers to learn from data and make predictions, or take actions without being explicitly programmed. By harnessing the vast amounts of information generated by our interconnected world, machine learning algorithms can identify patterns, extract insights, and drive decision-making with unprecedented accuracy and speed.

AI, often regarded as the pinnacle of technological achievement, goes beyond machine learning, encompassing the broader spectrum of intelligent systems capable of simulating human-like behaviors. From natural language processing and computer vision to robotics and expert systems, AI has evolved to replicate and augment human intelligence in astonishing ways.

The impact of machine learning and AI extends far beyond academia and research laboratories. These technologies are already revolutionizing industries, such as healthcare, finance, transportation, and manufacturing. Through automation, predictive analytics, and personalized experiences, businesses are leveraging machine learning and AI to gain a competitive edge and enhance their operations. The following trends can be recognized from the current field of machine learning and AI:

- **Deep learning and neural networks**: Deep learning has gained immense popularity in recent years and continues to be a dominant trend in machine learning and AI. Neural networks with multiple layers have proven to be highly effective in tasks such as image and speech recognition, natural language processing, and autonomous driving. The future will witness advancements in architectures, optimization techniques, and model interpretability, enabling even more complex and accurate predictions.

- **Reinforcement learning**: Reinforcement learning, a branch of machine learning that involves training agents to interact with an environment and learn through trial and error, has seen significant progress. Future trends in reinforcement learning will focus on tackling more complex and realistic scenarios, such as robotics, industrial automation, and game-playing. Advancements in algorithms and techniques, including model-based reinforcement learning and meta-learning, will enhance the capabilities of autonomous systems.

- **Edge computing and federated learning**: With the proliferation of **Internet of Things (IoT)** devices and the need for real-time decision-making, edge computing is gaining momentum. Edge devices, such as smartphones and IoT sensors, are equipped with the processing power to enable on-device machine learning. Federated learning, a distributed approach to training machine learning models on decentralized data, will be crucial to preserving privacy and scalability in edge computing environments, since it allows data to stay on edge devices, thus protecting user privacy and complying with data regulations.

- **Explainable AI and ethical considerations**: As machine learning and AI technologies become more embedded in our lives, there is a growing need for transparency and explainability. Explainable AI techniques aim to provide insights into how models make decisions, enabling users to understand and trust the outcomes. Additionally, ethical considerations, such as fairness, accountability, and bias mitigation, will play a pivotal role in shaping the future of machine learning and AI, ensuring responsible and ethical deployment of these technologies.

- **Generative models and unsupervised learning**: Generative models, such as **generative adversarial networks (GANs)** and **variational autoencoders (VAEs)**, have demonstrated remarkable capabilities in generating realistic images, text, and even music. Unsupervised learning, where models learn patterns and structures in data without explicit labels, holds great potential to discover hidden insights and reduce the dependency on labeled data. Future advancements in generative models and unsupervised learning will unlock new possibilities in creativity, data synthesis, and anomaly detection.

- **Augmented intelligence and human-AI collaboration**: The future of machine learning and AI is not solely about replacing humans but, rather, augmenting human capabilities. Augmented intelligence aims to combine the strengths of humans and machines, enabling collaborative decision-making and amplifying human expertise. This trend will emphasize human-centric design, user-friendly interfaces, and interactive AI systems that empower individuals in various domains, from healthcare and finance to creativity and scientific research.

- **Quantum machine learning**: Quantum computing, although still in its early stages, holds promise to solve complex problems that are beyond the reach of classical computers. Quantum machine learning algorithms are being developed to leverage quantum properties and accelerate computations, paving the way for advancements in drug discovery, optimization, cryptography, and other fields. The future will witness the intersection of quantum computing and machine learning, opening new avenues for innovation and breakthroughs.

The current and future trends of machine learning and AI reflect a rapidly evolving landscape that presents both exciting opportunities and challenges. From deep learning and reinforcement learning to edge computing and explainable AI, these trends are driving innovation, transforming industries, and shaping our future. With an emphasis on ethics, collaboration, and responsible deployment, the future of machine learning and AI holds the potential to create a more intelligent, efficient, and inclusive world.

Neglecting ethics, collaboration, and responsibility in AI development can lead to a range of negative consequences. These include the perpetuation of bias and discrimination, privacy violations through mishandling of personal data, a lack of accountability for developers and systems, potential safety hazards in applications such as autonomous vehicles, job displacement without proper workforce planning, AI making decisions without human oversight, security threats from vulnerable AI systems, difficulties for users in understanding AI decision-making, social unrest due to ethical concerns, and potential international tensions and conflicts related to AI advancements and ethics.

Now that we have familiarized ourselves with some of the potential megatrends and the direction of machine learning and AI, we will look at how to predict megatrends and how to evaluate whether technological advancement will become one. This will give you an edge to respond in a first frontier and take advantage of the new technology immediately.

How to recognize potential megatrends

A megatrend refers to a long-term and pervasive shift or pattern that has a significant impact on society, the economy, and various aspects of human life. Megatrends are powerful forces that shape the world we live in and often have far-reaching consequences, spanning multiple industries, regions, and generations. They typically unfold over decades and can influence technological advancements, cultural norms, economic systems, and social structures.

Megatrends are characterized by their broad and enduring impact, as well as their ability to bring about transformative changes. They reflect underlying shifts in demographics, technology, environmental factors, values, and global dynamics. Megatrends can influence consumer behavior, business strategies, policy-making, and societal norms, driving innovation, shaping markets, and creating new opportunities or challenges.

To get the full benefit of a rising megatrend, you should be at the frontier of recognizing the change to come. Recognizing megatrends requires a combination of observation, analysis, and an understanding of various factors influencing society, technology, economics, and demographics. The following principles can be applied to recognize potential megatrends:

- **Stay informed**: Keep yourself updated on the latest news, research, and developments in different fields. Follow reliable sources of information, including industry reports, academic publications, and expert opinions. Attend conferences, seminars, and webinars related to areas of interest to gain insights into emerging trends.

- **Analyze historical data**: Look at historical data and trends to identify patterns and understand the trajectory of past megatrends. Examine the impact of technological advancements, shifts in consumer behavior, regulatory changes, and other influential factors that have shaped major trends in the past.

- **Monitor societal and cultural shifts**: Pay attention to shifts in societal and cultural norms, values, and attitudes. Changes in demographics, lifestyle preferences, and social dynamics often indicate emerging megatrends. Study the evolving needs and aspirations of different generations and diverse populations to identify potential drivers of change.

- **Study technological advancements**: Technology is a key driver of megatrends. Keep a close watch on breakthrough technologies and innovations in various fields, such as AI, biotechnology, renewable energy, robotics, and quantum computing. Understand the potential implications and transformative power of these technologies in shaping future trends.

- **Consider economic and geopolitical factors**: Analyze economic indicators, global trade patterns, and geopolitical dynamics to identify potential megatrends. Factors such as economic growth, income inequality, resource scarcity, political stability, and international relations can significantly influence long-term trends.

- **Look for convergence and interconnections**: Megatrends often arise from the convergence of multiple factors and their interconnections. Explore how different domains, industries, and technologies intersect and interact with each other. Identify areas where advancements in one field can catalyze transformative changes in others.

- **Seek cross-disciplinary perspectives**: Embrace a multidisciplinary approach to gain a comprehensive understanding of megatrends. Engage with experts and professionals from diverse fields, including science, technology, economics, sociology, and psychology. Foster discussions and collaborations to gain different perspectives and insights.

- **Identify long-term shifts**: Megatrends are characterized by their long-term nature and enduring impact. Look for trends that have the potential to reshape industries, societies, and even global systems over extended periods. Focus on shifts that are likely to have sustained influence and create significant opportunities or challenges.

- **Anticipate future needs and challenges**: Identify emerging needs, problems, and challenges that society will face in the future. Anticipate how technological, social, and economic trends can address or exacerbate these issues. Megatrends often emerge as responses to pressing problems or changing demands.

- **Connect the dots**: Finally, connect the various pieces of information and observations to identify overarching themes and megatrends. Look for recurring patterns, commonalities, and signals that point toward long-term transformative changes. Develop a holistic understanding of the complex interactions between different factors to recognize and validate megatrends.

Examples of megatrends

Globalization: Globalization is the trend of increased interconnectedness and interdependence of countries through trade, investment, technology, and cultural exchange. It has led to a more interconnected world economy, with expanded trade and multinational corporations. Economic impacts include higher economic growth and supply chain integration. Geopolitically, it has resulted in trade tensions, resource competition, and shifting power dynamics among nations. Globalization drove international trade, investment, and the integration of global supply chains, resulting in heightened economic growth and the emergence of multinational corporations. It also reshaped geopolitical dynamics by altering power structures, international alliances, and competition for resources. Societies experienced cultural exchange, immigration, and the benefits of economic growth, yet also grappled with income inequality and cultural tensions.

Digitalization and technology advancements: This megatrend encompasses the rapid advancement of digital technologies and their integration into various aspects of society and the economy. It has led to technological innovation, productivity gains, and the emergence of new industries. Economically, it has driven growth and transformed sectors such as information technology. Geopolitically, it has sparked competition between nations for technological dominance, raised cybersecurity concerns, and prompted discussions on data governance and privacy. Digitalization fueled technological innovation, leading to increased productivity and the creation of entirely new industries. It empowered tech giants and transformed economic landscapes. Debates on data governance, privacy, and intellectual property rights took center stage. Society has become more connected and reliant on digital technology, presenting both opportunities and challenges.

Overall impact and interplay: The interplay between globalization and digitalization facilitated a global networked economy, allowing businesses to reach customers worldwide and enabling seamless information flow. This convergence led to rapid innovation, disruptively transforming traditional industries. However, it also introduced vulnerabilities, such as cybersecurity threats and data privacy concerns. The global ecosystem adapted, with digitalization supporting sustainable practices and green technologies, making environmental concerns central to economic and geopolitical discussions.

Remember that recognizing megatrends is not an exact science, and there is always an element of uncertainty involved. It requires a combination of research, critical thinking, and intuition to identify and understand the potential megatrends that will shape our future.

Once you have recognized a potential megatrend, you should be able to evaluate its potential importance. Evaluating the importance of a megatrend involves assessing its potential impact, scale, and long-term relevance. The following key factors should be considered when evaluating the importance of a megatrend:

- **Scale and reach**: Consider the scale and reach of the megatrend. Is it a global phenomenon or more localized? Careful analysis, research, and ongoing monitoring are essential to make accurate determinations regarding the global or localized nature of a megatrend. Does it affect multiple industries, sectors, or demographic groups? A megatrend with a wide-scale impact is generally more important, as it can shape the overall trajectory of societies, economies, and industries.

- **Duration and persistence**: Evaluate the expected duration and persistence of the megatrend. Predicting the precise duration of a megatrend is inherently uncertain, and many factors can influence its longevity. Megatrends are characterized by their long-term nature and enduring influence. A trend that is expected to last for decades or beyond is typically more important, as it can have sustained effects on various aspects of life.

- **Transformative potential**: Assess the transformative potential of the megatrend. Does it have the capacity to bring about significant changes, disrupt existing systems, and create new opportunities or challenges? Megatrends that can reshape industries, technologies, or societal structures are usually more important, as they can lead to major shifts in the way we live and work.

- **Economic impact**: Consider the economic implications of the megatrend. How does it affect economic systems, business models, and market dynamics? Megatrends that drive significant economic growth, create new markets, or shape consumer behavior are often deemed important, due to their impact on financial stability, job creation, and wealth distribution. For example, the "green energy transition" megatrend illustrates how global shifts toward cleaner energy practices drive economic growth, open new markets, and influence consumer behavior. This transition has led to the rapid growth of renewable energy industries, spawned new markets such as electric vehicles and energy storage, and shaped consumer choices toward sustainability. It not only addresses environmental concerns but also contributes to job creation, wealth distribution, and financial stability, showcasing the significant impact of megatrends on economies and societies.

- **Societal and cultural influence**: Evaluate the megatrend's influence on societal norms, values, and cultural practices. Does it shape behaviors, attitudes, or social structures? Megatrends that have a profound effect on cultural practices, social interactions, or value systems are considered important, as they can influence the fabric of society.

- **Interconnectedness**: Consider the interconnectedness of the megatrend with other trends and domains. Does it interact with or amplify other influential factors? Megatrends that have strong connections with other megatrends or can act as catalysts for additional trends tend to be more important, as they can create synergistic effects and drive further changes. Examples of strongly connected megatrends are urbanization and digitalization. Together, they influence the development and transformation of cities, economies, and societies, with implications for how people live, work, and interact in urban environments.

- **Long-term relevance**: Evaluate the long-term relevance and sustainability of the megatrend. Is it likely to remain significant and impactful in the future, or will it lose relevance over time? Megatrends that are expected to remain important and adaptive to changing circumstances are more valuable in shaping strategies and decision-making.

- **Expert consensus**: Consider the opinions and insights of experts, researchers, and industry leaders. Engage with individuals who have a deep understanding of the megatrend and its implications. Expert consensus and expert opinions can provide valuable perspectives to evaluate the importance and potential of a megatrend.

It is important to note that evaluating the importance of a megatrend involves some degree of uncertainty, as the future is inherently unpredictable. Therefore, ongoing monitoring and reassessment are essential, in order to adapt to changing circumstances and identify emerging megatrends that may supersede or intersect with existing ones.

Summary

In this chapter, we took a brief look at the future of machine learning and AI. These transformative technologies have captivated the world's imagination and hold the power to reshape societies and industries in profound ways. We explored the current and future trends in machine learning and AI, shedding light on the potential they hold to drive innovation and revolutionize various sectors.

Recognizing the importance of megatrends is crucial, and we provided a roadmap in this chapter to identify and evaluate these transformative shifts. By staying informed, analyzing historical data, monitoring societal shifts, studying technological advancements, and considering economic and geopolitical factors, we can gain valuable insights into the potential impact of megatrends.

As we look toward the future, our aim is to navigate the complexities of machine learning and AI, unravel their intricacies, and envision their potential impact on various aspects of our lives. By understanding these trends and recognizing the emergence of megatrends, we can harness the power of these technologies and shape a future that is intelligent, inclusive, and sustainable.

We started this chapter by getting some insights about the current and future trends in machine learning and AI. Then, we examined how to recognize and evaluate potential megatrends and how to gain the full benefits from them.

Index

W

waterfall charts 182, 183

X

XGBoost 49

Z

Z-score normalization 10

Packtpub.com

Subscribe to our online digital library for full access to over 7,000 books and videos, as well as industry leading tools to help you plan your personal development and advance your career. For more information, please visit our website.

Why subscribe?

- Spend less time learning and more time coding with practical eBooks and Videos from over 4,000 industry professionals

- Improve your learning with Skill Plans built especially for you

- Get a free eBook or video every month

- Fully searchable for easy access to vital information

- Copy and paste, print, and bookmark content

Did you know that Packt offers eBook versions of every book published, with PDF and ePub files available? You can upgrade to the eBook version at packtpub.com and as a print book customer, you are entitled to a discount on the eBook copy. Get in touch with us at customercare@packtpub.com for more details.

At www.packtpub.com, you can also read a collection of free technical articles, sign up for a range of free newsletters, and receive exclusive discounts and offers on Packt books and eBooks.

Other Books You May Enjoy

If you enjoyed this book, you may be interested in these other books by Packt:

Hands-On Business Intelligence with Qlik Sense

Pablo Labbe, Clever Anjos, Kaushik Solanki, Jerry DiMaso

ISBN: 978-1-78980-094-4

- Discover how to load, reshape, and model data for analysis
- Apply data visualization practices to create stunning dashboards
- Make use of Python and R for advanced analytics
- Perform geo-analysis to create visualizations using native objects
- Learn how to work with AGGR and data stories

Mastering Qlik Sense

Juan Ignacio Vitantonio, Martin Mahler

ISBN: 978-1-78355-402-7

- Understand the importance of self-service analytics and the IKEA-effect

- Explore all the available data modeling techniques and create efficient and optimized data models

- Master security rules and translate permission requirements into security rule logic

- Familiarize yourself with different types of Master Key Item(MKI) and know how and when to use MKI.

- Script and write sophisticated ETL code within Qlik Sense to facilitate all data modeling and data loading techniques

- Get an extensive overview of which APIs are available in Qlik Sense and how to take advantage of a technology with an API

- Develop basic mashup HTML pages and deploy successful mashup projects

Packt is searching for authors like you

If you're interested in becoming an author for Packt, please visit `authors.packtpub.com` and apply today. We have worked with thousands of developers and tech professionals, just like you, to help them share their insight with the global tech community. You can make a general application, apply for a specific hot topic that we are recruiting an author for, or submit your own idea.

Share Your Thoughts

Now you've finished *Machine Learning with Qlik Sense*, we'd love to hear your thoughts! Scan the QR code below to go straight to the Amazon review page for this book and share your feedback or leave a review on the site that you purchased it from.

`https://packt.link/r/1-805-12615-6`

Your review is important to us and the tech community and will help us make sure we're delivering excellent quality content.

Download a free PDF copy of this book

Thanks for purchasing this book!

Do you like to read on the go but are unable to carry your print books everywhere? Is your eBook purchase not compatible with the device of your choice?

Don't worry, now with every Packt book you get a DRM-free PDF version of that book at no cost.

Read anywhere, any place, on any device. Search, copy, and paste code from your favorite technical books directly into your application.

The perks don't stop there, you can get exclusive access to discounts, newsletters, and great free content in your inbox daily

Follow these simple steps to get the benefits:

1. Scan the QR code or visit the link below

https://packt.link/free-ebook/978-1-80512-615-7

2. Submit your proof of purchase

3. That's it! We'll send your free PDF and other benefits to your email directly

www.ingramcontent.com/pod-product-compliance
Lightning Source LLC
LaVergne TN
LVHW081522050326
832903LV00025B/1588

* 9 7 8 1 8 0 5 1 2 6 1 5 7 *